IOWA'S VANISHING OUT HOUSE

by

Bruce Carlson

QUIXOTE PRESS
R.R. #4, Box 33B
Blvd. Station
Sioux City, Iowa
51109

i

**QUIXOTE
PRESS**
Bruce Carlson
R.R. #4, Box 33B
Blvd. Station
Sioux City, Iowa
51109

DEDICATION

This book is dedication to all those Iowans who have rushed down those familiar paths to the outhouse on a cold night, only too anxious to get back to the warmth and comfort of their beds.

The author wants to thank all those who have shared photographs and information with him to make this book possible.

He wants to thank those who have told of memories about incidents that made the Iowa outhouse an important part of their lives.

TABLE OF CONTENTS

FORWARD 9

PREFACE 11

CHAPTERS
    I   The Salesman 13
    II   Only Six Feet 23
   III Why The Quarter Moon? 29
   IV The Big Moment 33
    V   The Great Smoked Ham Escapade .41
   VI Twelve of 'Em 49
   VII Trapped 55
  VIII Laura's Revenge 61
   IX Those Dang Boys 69
    X   The Attack .77
   XI The Homemade Earthquake 85
   XII A Plan That Backfired 93
  XIII The Beehive 99
  XIV Remodeling The Outhouse 105
   XV The Stone Outhouse 111
  XVI The Lock Up 117
  XVII Reduced To Ashes 125
 XVIII The Outhouse Issue 131
  XIX Outwitted In An Outhouse 139
   XX Vincent's Bad Day 145
  XXI Repossession 151
  XXII The Electric Fence 153

EPILOGUE 159

INDEX 165

FOREWARD

The human experience is strewn with artifacts, institutions and ideas that have each served their purpose, then faded into obscurity. These have varied from the trivial to the notable, and from the base to the noble.

Such has been the lot of the outhouses here in Iowa. Someday the last outhouse in the state will be pushed into a creek or fall victim to a bonfire. That day will be both as important and as unnoticed as the day the first outhouse was built among the prairie grasses of "The Land Between the Rivers." Drum rolls and the waving of flags will no more accompany the demise of the last then they did the birth of the first. It will happen quietly. Most ideas come and go that way, you know.

The end of the outhouse is probably a good thing. We have better ways now. However, those of us who have lived with The-Little-House-Out-Back will always have a little warm spot in our hearts for that ugly little structure. If nothing else, it sure did a great job of making us appreciate indoor plumbing.

Professor Phil Hey
Brair Cliff College
Sioux City, Iowa

PREFACE

This is a book about the vanishing outhouses of Iowa. It has some photographs, illustrations and stories about those little houses out back that have played such a pivotal role in the lives of earlier Iowans.

Some of the outhouses spoken of in this book are still in use, but many now serve no more important function than sheltering things, like fence posts, that really don't need to be sheltered. Some are reduced to being a roosting place for sparrows, or simply lean against a nearby boxelder tree, jus' kinda tired, ya know.

I suppose that, someday, the Privius Americanus that ranged the prairies of Iowa will find itself in a museum where passers-by can look at it among the other relics. But today there are still a few tucked away among the trees and buildings of Iowa's farmsteads. If you want your child or grandchild to see a real live Privius Americans, you had better hurry. They are a vanishing species.

Skip McQuire's Pride and Joy

CHAPTER I

THE SALESMAN

 his is an account of the experience of a harness salesman from Buffalo, New York, and the difficulties he had with his boss. He almost lost his job as a result of an Iowa outhouse in 1896.

Apparently this salesman hadn't been long in the employment of the Erie Leather Goods Company when the whole mess transpired. He had gotten that job only after literally begging for it. This man had a long history of alcohol dependency. Of course, that's not what they called it back then, but that's what his pro-

blem was. He had lost more than one job because of that and had landed the job with Erie Leather Goods only through the intervention of his brother-in-law who was an officer of the company. His brother-in-law's boss hadn't been keen on the

idea of hiring Charles so he knew he was on trial. He knew that if he messed up, he'd be gone. Old Demon Rum had just about done a number on Charles so this was about his last chance at a decent job anywhere.

Charles' route was in central Iowa. He called only on retail stores rather than on individuals so that large territory worked out alright. He did, of course, spend many many hours on the road.

It was a pleasant job. For one thing, the company had set him up with a fine rig and a handsome team to pull it. They had fixed that team up with about the grandest-looking set of harness a body

could hope to see. The company wanted their accounts to knew what a realy good harness could look like. When Charles pulled into an inn with that outfit, he'd get real good service. All in all, it was a fine job.

The other principal player in this tale was a farmer by the name of "Skip" McQuire. Skip's place was a bit north of Boone, in those hills along the Des Moines River.

Skip was not only a farmer, but a bit of a inventor. His place was crawling with numerous embodiments of his creativity and mechanical skills. Mrs. McQuire often teased Skip about that and told him that he farmed only as an excuse to build countless devices to make his work easier or, at least, more fun.

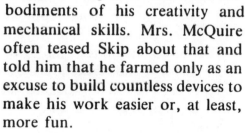

One of Skip's inventions consisted of a rigged-up outhouse. He had, near the base of the structure, a pair of wagon wheels on an axle that was, in turn, bolted onto the rear of the outhouse. Rising up from the center of that axle was a long pole. Skip was right proud of his outhouse. All he had to do was to pull the top of that pole down toward the ground, and Presto!, he'd have an outhouse on wheels. When it came time to move the outhouse, it was a simple job of rolling it to the next site.

Like everything else on the place, Skip kept his outhouse in good shape, even going so far as to keeping the wheel bearings well greased. A neighbor often teased Skip about his always taking the wheels off the outhouse and checking that grease. The neighbor never tired of pointing out that that outhouse probably wouldn't travel a total of half a mile in all of Skip's life. Skip was to eventually wish that he hadn't greased those bearing so well.

Skip's life and that of Charles, the harness salesman, were to cross paths in September of 1896. It was then that Skip had decided to move that outhouse. He had dug a new pit for it and figured he'd do that job after chore time. He knew it would take just a few minutes, what with that set of wheels and all.

Well, you know how that can go. He ran into some delay at chore time and didn't get to the outhouse moving job until it was starting to get dark.

That was no real problem, though. He didn't have far to move it and he could see well with the aid of a lantern his wife held for him.

Ol' Skip pulled that long handle down and proceeded to push the building the few yards to the new pit. His lantern failed, however, to warn him of a shovel laying there on the ground. Skip stumbled over that dang shovel, and dropped the handle on that outhouse. Everything that could have gone wrong did. Being on a sidehill, and all, that outhouse started rolling. The dragging top end of the handle offered enough resistance that the rig didn't just wheel around in little circles as a two-wheeled vehicle is apt to do. It took off straight down the hill, those well-greased bearings doing their thing.

By the time the outhouse got to the fence around the yard, it was going fast enough that it simply crashed right on through it. There was nothing between that runaway outhouse and the road now except  several hundred yards of good smooth going. That trip down the hill provided the time for the structure to really get up a good head of steam. The sheriff later estimated that the outhouse must have been doing a good twenty to twenty-five miles an hour by the time it got to the bottom of the hill down there on the road.

Meanwhile, down on that road Charles, the harness salesman, was on his way to Boone to spend the night. Charles was sober as a judge and looking forward to a nice clean bed for the night. He'd traveled quite a few miles that day, and the hour was getting late.

The rhythmic sounds of his team's hooves on the ground was a bit hypnotic, especially since Charles was tired anyway. He wasn't paying a whole lot of attention to things around him in the darkness of that September night. He had but a couple of seconds warning before his whole world seemed to come apart. Suddenly he heard a swishing sort of sound. The next instant he and his buggy were rolling end over end. At the same time, his terrified horses were pulling the buggy along the ground at a terrible rate. Charles soon found himself terribly shaken, but unhurt, lying in the ditch with what was left of his buggy draped around him. Somewhere down the road was his team running away with over three hundred dollars worth of fancy harness on them. A few yards away was an outhouse with its wheels up in the air and still spinning.

It took a few moments for Charles, in his dazed state, to even realize that what he was seeing was an outhouse. An outhouse on wheels was enough of a shock, but a runaway outhouse that had just crashed into him was even harder to figure out. Somethin' was certain sure crazy going on, and Charles knew that somehow, he was a victim of it all.

As Charles extracted himself from the remains of

his buggy, up rushed Skip McQuire who had run down that long hill in pursuit of his outhouse.

"Are ya all right, Mister?" asked a puffing and huffing Skip McQuire.

What with Charles' heart in his throat, he found it hard to talk at first. His mouth got to working for a minute before he could make any words come out.

"Yeah, I'm alright, but my buggy ain't, and my team has done run off. Who are you and what happened? What in the tarnation is that rig layin' over there in the ditch with the wheels still 'a going' around?"

As the pair walked up the hill to Skip's house, Skip spent about half the trip apologizing to Charles and the other half asking if he was alright. During a round of coffee and biscuits to calm Charles down, Skip explained the whole thing. He explained how that outhouse got away from him and how sorry about it and all he was.

Skip harnessed up his own team and the pair set off to track down that runaway team of Charles's. They found them about a mile and a half down the road calming grazing along the grassy roadside. One of them had almost no harness left on him and other's was damaged badly.

The two men corralled the horses and gave them some oats and water. Skip put Charles up there at the house for what was left of the night.

Charles was, of course, worried stiff that the episode would prove to be the end of his employment with 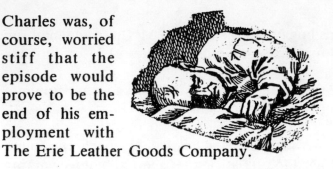 The Erie Leather Goods Company.

In the morning, Charles was offered all the comforts of home, except, of course, an outhouse. Skip didn't have to explain why they didn't have an outhouse. The reason was abundantly obvious. Mrs. McQuire was a bit edgy over the fact that they were fresh out of outhouses, too, of course. She made that point rather clear with the remark:

"It seems that folks that don't have a fancy feature like wheels on their outhouses still manage to have an outhouse when they need 'em."

The next day Charles sent a report right away, by mail to his boss. He had to report the loss of the buggy, some gear, the harness, and an injured leg on one of the horses. He so reported all that on a form provided by the company in case of an accident or loss by other means. When it came to the part about what had caused the loss, Charles simply put "collision with a runaway outhouse."

Charles should have elaborated a bit on that explanation. It was quite obvious to his boss, when he got the report, that Charles was drunk.

The boss stormed into Charles' brother-in-law's office with the report in hand.

"It's clear to me that that man was not only drunk when he wrecked our property but hadn't sobered up yet when he wrote out this report. That's the end of him and I don't want any more of your relatives coming around here looking for a job."

A wire was sent to a company representative in Des Moines who immediately went to hunt the guilty salesman down. His job was to tell him that he was fired.

Fortunately, however, Skip McQuire was willing to testify as to what had happened and that it wasn't Charles's fault. He provided the man from Des Moines with a letter to that effect. He testified that Charles was stone sober at the time of the accident and that it wasn't his fault at all.

The whole mess didn't cost Charles his job after all, but it cost Skip McQuire plenty. He paid for a buggy, some rather expensive harness, board and room for a sick horse for a month, and one mobile outhouse.

The Halloween Trap

CHAPTER II

ONLY SIX FEET

his potograph shows a kind of ordinary outhouse that occupies a corner of the yard on a farm not too far west of Davenport. That outhouse represents, to me the use of a simple solution to solve a difficult problem back in the 1920s.

The problem was one facing this structure's owner, Jim Holland. Like others in Iowa, and elsewhere, the outhouse was faced with the annual hazards of Halloween. Every Halloween night it would have to suffer the same indignity. Some of the local young men would tip it over. It was always the same, those scoundrels would come up behind the thing, rush at it, and knock it over so it lay on its front.

Twice Jim saw the fellows actually do the dirty deed. They'd come rushing out of the neighboring timber and throw themselves against the back wall of the outhouse. Then they'd be gone as quickly as they had arrived.

Jim had a fair idea as to who a couple of the fellows were but couldn't prove it. He'd have loved to have the necessary proof so's to make it good and hot for them. It just plain wasn't any fun having to prop that old outhouse up again every year. Those annual falls were proving to be a bit tough on the building. The two-by-fours were starting to loosen up a bit and the roof had already gotten a bit crooked.

Jim was complaining to his neighbor about the problem and how he wished he wouldn't be faced with that problem every year.

"Those dang boys come a sneakin' up behind that thing every Halloween and pitch it forward. I seed 'em twice do it. They jus' come a rushin' out of the timber and throw theirselves at that back wall. You take four or five husky boys a doin' that, and it tends ta weaken an outhouse up, ya know."

The neighbor came up with an idea.

"Why don't ya jus' move the outhouse six foot forward as soon as it gets dark come Halloween night? Beings kind of out in the open away from that timber a few yards, the boys might not never notice it's moved. When it gets dark, things kind of look different anyways, ya know."

As the readers knows, there's nothing really very distasteful about an outhouse. It isn't the building itself that's objectionable. It's that pit underneath that we'd rather not think about. Well, moving that building a few feet forward left that pit just behind it of course. Jim was real proud of his neighbor's suggestion and put his plan into operation as soon as Halloween arrived and it got a bit dark. Even Jim could hardly tell there in the darkness, that the building was a bit out of place.

Jim had always dreaded Halloween, but this time he found himself looking forward to it and to sweet revenge. He was ready for 'em now. Let 'em come rushin' out of that timber and throw themselves again that back wall. They'd have a surprise in store for 'em this time.

Jim started to get worried along about 10:30 that night. He had positioned himself out in the garage waiting there in the darkness for his tormentors. He had set himself up with a nice comfortable chair and a cup of coffee along with a bag of donuts. He'd chuckle to himself now and then as he savored his coming revenge.

(25)

Then, almost without any warning, it happened. He heard some cracking of twigs in the timber just before he made out the image of five stout fellows hurtling across those few yards from the timber to the outhouse. A donut half way to Jim's mouth hesistated there a few moments as he watched the drama unfold.

Those unsuspecting boys didn't know what hit 'em. Four of the five were in that pit, the fifth escaped only because he had stumbled before getting to the building. His clumsiness saved him from a fate his companions never forgot. The half-obscured sight he saw there in the darkness was one that told him his buddies were in lots and lots of trouble.

There were some mightly upset parents that night when those boys came home with abundant evidence about them of what they had been up to.

Some of the boys' clothes were burned that night and some the following morning. Jim Holland noted several bonfires throughout the neighborhood with a certain degree of satisfaction. He decided that Halloween was all right after all. He heard from one friend that one of the fellows had been wearing a brand new pair of $20 boots. Apparently those boots joined that fellow's other clothes in the bonfire

they had at that house. Twenty dollars for a pair of boots back in the '20s was no small amount of course. Yes, Halloween was alright!

A really ironic twist to the whole affair was that one of those hastily contrived bonfires caught the culprit's shed on fire and leveled it.

There was some talk of retaliation against Jim Holland, but apparently those fellows decided they had had enough of that guy to last the rest of their lives.

The Quarter-Moon

CHAPTER III

WHY THE QUARTER-MOON?

t's kind of difficult to work the subject into polite conversation, but when the issue comes up, you'll be ready for it after reading this chapter.

The history of the quarter-moon on the door of the outhouse goes way back. Most serious historians who are students of the subject are of the opinion that the custom started in Europe in the 1500s or the 1600s.

It was common practice, back then, to identify which outhouse was which by means of a circular symbol on the door of the mens' and a quarter-moon on the ladies'. The use of symbols rather than words was necessary due to the widespread illiteracy of the times. When a feller can't read and is headed for the outhouse, he sure doesn't need some incomprehensible hieorglyphics on the door to figure out.

The circular symbol and the quarter-moon were Europe's version of the Chinese Yin and Yang. The circle was representative of the sun which symbolized masculinity. The more subdued and submissive moon, on the other hand, represented femininity. (This isn't my idea, ladies. I'm jus' reporting the situation as it was back then.)

The use of the circle and quarter-moon was especially common at inns and houses for lodging. Not only was illiteracy a problem, but also the clientele of such places was more likely to be travelers from another country and another language.

These universal signs were easy to make and easy to "read," so most such places had the little houses out back so designated, one with a circular sign, and one with the quarter-moon.

So why is the quarter-moon applied in more recent times to outhouses in general?

The answer to that apparently lies in the economics of maintaining outhouses. If one of the outhouses at an inn, for example, were to have fallen into a state of disrepair, the solution was often to transfer, if necessary, the quarter moon onto the surviving structure. It was reasoned that the men could always simply step out into the shadows of the tress. An outhouse had to be kept for the ladies, of course, so whatever outhouse fell apart first was automatically the men's.

This practice became so widespread that in many many cases, only a women's outhouse would be available to those who frequented such public places. Since those carried the quarter-moon, that symbol soon evolved into the sign for any outhouse in general rather than one for ladies only.

Now, aren't you glad you know that?

Right Where It Shoulda Stayed

CHAPTER IV

THE BIG MOMENT

his is a story out of my own boyhood in those Loess Hills north of Sioux City back in the middle 1940s.

Dad was a physician and had his office in town. His quite properly modern office hid from his patients and his colleagues, the real nature of Dr. Carlson. He was a farm boy through and through. His hours there in Sioux City were simply those intervals between spells of living his real life. Real life, to Dad, was living on that patch of hills just like his father had lived there before him.

We not only had the mandatory outhouse, but also the horse-drawn equipment for the little farming we did. We had the bucket setting on the table there in the kitchen. That bucket had to be run down to the spring by the creek frequently to get filled. That chore was, unfortunately, done by means of boy power. Yes, we had all the paraphernalia and practices of the same life that Dad's father had lived there on that place.

Oh, I knew well enough about things like running water and tractors. It was just that those sort of things were what other people had. All that was hard on Mother, of course. For me, however, it was just the way it was.

I wasted my time at the near-by country school between doing the important stuff like rabbit hunting and simply wandering around in those beautiful hills.

My life was pretty well bounded and defined by those three ranges of hills that dominated the skyline around our place. That was a big enough world for me and suited me just fine.

Dad had one obvious characteristic that anyone who knew him could see. He had to manage everything; all in full detail. He had to do this with as big an audience as possible, and with the greatest amount of noise that any given situation could drum up. He liked having guinia hens and geese around for they would set up a big commotion at the slightest provocation. Geese and guinia hens were his kind of people.

If Dad couldn't run something, it just simply wasn't worth running. That need to be at the helm of every project included the moving of the outhouse on August day in 1944.

That morning, before going to town. Dad left the hired man and myself with very explicit and detailed instructions for the outhouse moving project. Its capacity was exhausted and it was time for that operation again. Dad being Dad, he couldn't trust Old Oscar and me to do that actual moving job. We were fit only to get things ready. He told us to dig the pit, harness up the horses, and line up the necessary rope and chain in readiness for his return. Only *he* could drive the team to drag that outhouse to its new pit. I recall Oscar complaining a bit about not being trusted to drive that team.

"Ya'd think a man could do that job hisself without havin' to wait fur someone else to do a simple little thing like pullin' a danged outhouse."

I, of course, knew my dad well enough that I knew there was no point in laboring over the issue. When it came to the glory stuff like the actual moving operation, Dad wasn't about to play any role but the lead one.

Our instructions were to dig that pit at a specific location about fifty feet from the current one. Dad had meticulously laid out exactly where that pit was to be and its dimensions. Our duty was to dig 'er.

So, under the watchful eye of those loess hills, Oscar and I labored long over that task. Our outhouse was a bit fancier than most, and Dad was right proud of it. We knew that a pit poorly dug would mean a pit redug. We knew he'd accept no shoddy workmanship like a pit of irregular shape or one with sloping walls. He'd have a pit worthy of that outhouse or know the reason why.

As Dad went off for town, there was that unspoken question left hanging. Were the two of us in charge worthy of digging that fine outhouse? Our mission was to prove that we were. Sometimes I had the distinct impression that Oscar was not properly sensitive to such cosmic issues as that.

I'd worry about Oscar, wondering if he really understood how Dad's projects were always much more important than the ordinary comings and goings of regular people.

When Dad got home, we were ready for him. The pit was dug, the chain and rope was all attached. Pearl and Nellie were hitched up, ready for the arrival of the Prima Donna of outhouse movers. All of us were ready for THE BIG MOMENT.

After enough shouted instructions, meaningful glances at the sky, and the dog and winged spectators were all properly hyped up for the occasion, Dad did it. He slapped those reins on the backs of Pearl and Nellie. The stately old outhouse started its journey to the new pit.

It was a perfect situation for Dad. There was lots of noise and excitement and he was right in the center of it all. All the shouting, barking, cackling, and the grunting of the horses was like music to his ears. It was one of those rare moments that made worthwhile all the inconveniences of living at the end of a half mile long mud road. The presence of Oscar and me, as well as that of my sister and mother who came out to witness the occasion plus a neighbor who happened by made for a nice audience. It was truly Dad's kind of moment.

(36)

The magic of the time was almost over as soon as it got started. There right before our eyes was the outhouse almost exactly positioned over the pit. I held my breath in excitement as I saw all those well-laid plans being fulfilled.

Then suddenly, time seemed to stand still. I remember first my mother making those short little gasps she would make when Dad swore. I recall my sister starting to giggle and a wide grin settled over Oscar's face. He was standing there with his hands on his hips as if everything was alright with the world.

The incogruity of seeing only the roof of the outhouse there on the ground was almost more than I could mentally absorb. It took a few moments for me to realize what had happened. That neat meticulously laid-out rectangle that Dad had scratched in the dust had somehow gone awry. Apparently he had mismeasured. The pit was a few inches too wide and about a foot too long. That pit wasn't neatly positioned under the outhouse. It had gobbled it up, leaving only the roof exposed. The overhang of the roof so neatly covered the narrow gap between the walls of the outhouse and the sides of the pit, it looked all in the world as if it was only the roof lying there on the ground. It was enough to shake a boy's faith in fathers, outhouses, and the natural order of things.

I don't know how many of you readers have ever attempted to extract a half ton of outhouse from a hole in the ground so small that there was no way to get a hold on the structure. Believe me, it was an engineering challenge. A solution was far beyond the capabilities of Oscar or myself. The women were of no help. Mother had stalked back into the house in protest over Dad's swearing. My sister had found that chasing the geese was more fun than watching three fellows standing around scratching their heads over the dilemima.

That challenge tested even Dad's ingenuity and found him wanting. After several hours of abortive attempts to get that building out of the ground, Dad made a dramatic announcement. Drastic circumstances demanded drastic solutions.

"Oscar, we'll burn 'er down. Light fire to that thing, and we'll build a new one."

I knew then why Dad was a leader of men. His ability to make such major decisions in the face of such adversity was truly mind-boggling.

Oh, we built a pretty good outhouse to replace the one that was simply reduced to a pile of ashes, but it didn't have the class the original one had. It was a little more boxy in appearance and didn't have some of the architectural details its predecessor had boasted.

A few days later while my sister and I were talking about the new outhouse, Dad was already making great plans for the next day.

"Now, Oscar, you and Bruce loosen up the planking on the bridge and when I get home from the office, we'll turn 'em all over and bolt 'em down again. Those old planks are getting to looking pretty scuffed up."

(38)

Later, Oscar was muttering something to me about that job.

"You'd think a man could turn a plank over hisself without waiting for your Old Man to come home."

I didn't say anything to Oscar about that. I knew there was no way to explain to him that neither he nor I would be able to set the tone for such an operation like Dad could. I knew that when Dad came home that night, that job would be done in fine style. Before it was over, he'd have the dog raising cain and the geese a hissin' and a flappin' their wings. Ya gotta approach such things as bridge plank turnin' with a certain degree of class, ya know.

The Dual Purpose Outhouse

CHAPTER V

THE GREAT SMOKED HAM ESCAPADE

 he outhouse pictured here was the cause of an incident that really stirred up a big fuss in the community west of Des Moines in 1918. It all started out innocently enough and no one really was of a mind to hassle anybody else. The whole thing just kind of grew out of one simple little act.

This outhouse was near a modest little house on a farm belonging to a family that wasn't exactly known for being overly concerned about cleaniness. They, in fact, were said to have been

the messiest people in the area. The folks in the community always managed to come up with some excuse not to have a meal at that farm. Most folks weren't what you'd call overy fussy, but they drew the line at eating at that place. They didn't know much about germs but figured they knew what they could or couldn't stomach. And they couldn't stomach the thought of eating there.

That situation sort of complicated the whole tradition of eating at the various homes when the threshing crews made their rounds. The issue came up the first year they were to thresh at the farm in question. What to do? No one was about to flat-out say they would't eat there, but everyone wanted out of it someway.

One of the ladies came up with a solution. She suggested that she and a couple of the other farm-wives could go to the lady of the offending house and offer to help tidy the place up a little bit in preparation for the big day when the threshing crew came.

"It would be only fair to help, don't ya know.?"

So that's what they did. They cleaned that house, especially the kitchen, like it'd never been cleaned before. It just shone. It was so clean, and everybody was real proud of that woman coming up with that idea.

Everyone knew that several other ladies would be there doing the cookin' so they'd keep a good eye on how things were done.

The big day came, along with all the men to do the threshing. After several hours of hot work in the fields, it was time for one of those monstrous threshing crew dinners. They all trooped into the

house in readiness for the fine dinner that was prepared under the watchful eyes of the various neighbor ladies. The men were all looking forward to "setting down" to what was very obviously a good meal.

As was the practice for such occasions, the table groaned under the burden of all the fine vittles. There were two  huge smoked hams, lots of hot 'taters 'n gravy, all kinds of fresh vegetables, and unlimited homemade pies and cakes. Out on the porch waited a mountain of homemade ice cream to be the dessert.

Even the dog lay over by the sink, content in the knowledge that when it was all over, there would be a bunch of leftover goodies for him.

The only thing in the meal that really came from the place was that pair of big old smoked hams. The other ladies weren't about to trust any cookin' to the hostess that could be messed up. They gently guided her into harmless chores like cutting the wood to feed that ravenous cookstove out in the summer kitchen.

During the course of the meal all sorts of things were discussed. Precedence was, of course, given to things like the weather, the price of oats, and what the no-good politicians were up to that year.

The whole unfortunate affair was set in motion by an innocent question one of the men asked in a lull in the conversation. He directed his question to the hostess.

"Who smoked the hams for ya, Ma'm?"

"Why, we smoked 'em right here on the place."

(44)

"But", the man replied. "I didn't know you had a smokehouse here on this farm. Did ya' build one after ya moved on.?"

"Oh, no. We don't have what you'd call a regular smokehouse. We jus' lit us a fire down under the outhouse and let 'er fill up with smoke. We jus' hung 'em out there in that outhouse."

The next few moments gave a new meaning to the word "silence." All the chatter stopped, and you could have heard a germ drop there in that dining room. All eyes turned to the lady of the house and the man asking the questions.

That fellow found a tiny sliver on his thumb he had to work on as he desperately tried to figure out some way out of the limelight.

The awkward silence was suddenly broken by a couple of "Well's and a "Well, I declare!" Two of the women and a man simply got up and went home. Others started to pull out their pocket watches to study them and to announce that "It was bearin' on toward chore time."

One old farmer didn't have a watch. In desperation, he studied the calendar hanging on the wall before announcing that he suddenly remembered he had a sick calf to tend to and he'd "best get going".

One woman firmly told her husband that they might have a sick calf too, so they best be on their way.

The treshin' crew dwindled right fast as the various members of it contemplated the situation.

There ended up, in the next few days, a lot of people mad at each other, and at the hostess and her husband. Even the woman who came up with the idea of going over there to clean the house up didn't escape critism. Some of the folks were mad at her. She, in turn, was mad at about everyone else. After all, ti was a good idea. She just didn't think about how that ham might have got cured.

There is no evidence that anyone in the crew suffered any disabling condition as a result of that meal. Maybe they were being a bit overly fussy after all.

As you can see in the photo, that broken-down old outhouse sure doesn't look like it has ever been anything but awfully ordinary.

(46)

There is nothing about it that suggests that it played such a pivotal role in The Great Smoked Ham Escapade of 1918.

The New Superintendent's Answer
To The Traveling Schoolhouse

CHAPTER VI

TWELVE OF 'EM

peaking of schools, we've grown so accustomed to thinking in terms of two outhouses for each country school, the idea of more than that seems odd.

Well, P.S. #2 in northeastern Iowa county had twelve of 'em! Oh, it started out with the normal two alright, but that soon grew to twelve, six each.

The reason for the twelve outhouses is an interesting one. Back in the 1880s, when all this took place, there was lots of dissension within the community served by P.S. #2 as to where that little schoolhouse should be located. There was the faction at the west end of the valley that held out for putting it up on a little knoll down there. Just as adamant were the farmers in the east who felt it should be up there. Other groups had their preferences, loudly voiced, of course. Amid all this turmoil the decision was made to place the building smack dab in the middle of the valley.

The westenders didn't take that lying down. They knew they had been cheated and wanted justice done. And what they called justice was, indeed, done one night with eight men and six teams of good horses. Those fellows jack-  ed that little building up, slid some poles under it to serve as skids, and hauled the schoolhouse down the valley to their little knoll. By chore time in the morning, that schoolhouse was all set up on the pretty little knoll along with two brand new outhouses.

Well, that made some of the folks mad for sure. Those people who had had the school in their neighborhood now found it about three miles away. The valley was in a real stir that next day.

Those *?#*&*!? westenders had done stole the

schoolhouse! Tempers were running high enough that day that two of the farmers stood guard on that knoll the first night to be sure their efforts weren't in vain. They sure didn't want the building to get moved again.

The eastenders had plenty of time to wait. In a few days, the hollering about the whole issue sort of died down. That's when the farmers in the east end struck. They gathered several teams together and during the wee hours, they drug that little schoolhouse off that knoll, on past its original site, and two miles further east. They figured that turnabout was fair play. They had 'em a schoolhouse right close by now. They too, added a couple of new outhouses and some play equipment. They even built a little fence around the yard by the time the sun peeked up over the horizon in the morning.

As expected, the whole thing sort of got out of hand. Other residents of the district solved their problem the same way. That schoolhouse was drug from site to site, depending on who was gettin' tired of having it so far away. Several times the children had to follow those skid marks in the road to track down the schoolhouse so they could go to their classes. On some occasions, the fellows kind of covered up the tracks and the poor kids couldn't find their school.

The teacher, Miss Annie Boggs, didn't much care where her school was. She got a bit out of sorts when she couldn't find it, though.

Apparently several of these warring factions found it more convenient to build outhouses at their sites than it was to move the other neighborhoods' outhouses. As a result, there ended up six complete sets of those little houses out back. The folks in that valley might not have had running water in their school house, but they had the next best thing; a running schoolhouse.

Rumor has it that the farmers in the valley plumb wore out three sets of skids before the issue was finally settled.

The traveling schoolhouse was finally rebuilt since all that moving pretty well broke it up. One wall had started to kind of buckle and most of the windows glasses got cracked as that building would be drug over one rutty road after another. The rebuilding was the idea of a new superintendent of schools that was elected in 1888. He took the job on the one condition that he would have the final say on where the schoolhouse would be put.

The man was assured by the various factions that he could have his say, and the building would stay wherever he said.

Just to be sure, however, the new building was made large enough and heavy enough that it was virtually impossible to marshall enough men and horses to move it. It was put right where the original one had been several years earlier. The best of the whole gang of outhouses were moved to the site, some of the poorest ones burned, and the rest were autioned off to individuals within the community.

The Outhouse that saved Bert William's Life

CHAPTER VII

TRAPPED

uth Williams who used to live at Carroll told me about an incident involving her uncle that almost ended in tragedy.

"Uncle Bert wasn't the most ambitious man in the world. That laziness probably was a good thing, though. It might be what saved his life one day."

Ruth started our conversation out that way when I was talking to her about a story she was supposed to have about the outhouse pictured on page 54. I'd always been kind of partial to laziness myself. I guess I always figured that laziness was its own reward, but here was a gal with a story about how

laziness had saved somebody's life. That certainly sounded like a story worth listening to. Ya never know when you can use a situation like that to refer to when you're having a discussion with your wife, you know.

Ruth went on to tell me about the incident involving her uncle. She explained, first, that her aunt and uncle's outhouse near Carroll was, like the other buildings on the place, a bit run-down.

"Aunt Ida used to hassle Uncle Bert to no end about fixing that shaky old thing up or building a new one. She said it looked so bad that it made the other buildings look halfway acceptable.

It seems that Bert was a lot less enthused about the outhouse project than his wife was. He found one reason or another to let that chore kind of get put off year after year.

The day he was really glad he did was in April of 1916. Bert had kind of raked some of the dead leaves and grass up from around the outhouse, and had him a little fire going  there in the early evening. He had thrown some old timbers he had stacked by the nearby shed on the fire and some other assorted junk. He ended up with a good little blaze and was sort of occupying his time leaning on his rake handle and watching the fire.

When Uncle Bert had occasion to step into the outhouse for a minute he noticed it was awfully unstable. He remembered, then, that he had loosened one of the stones holding up one side when he had been raking around it. His resolve to wait 'til the next day to replace that stone was an unfortunate one.

He happened to throw his weight against the door when he closed it behind him. That was just enough to send that outhouse tumbling off its remaining supports and over onto the ground.

Now, being in an outhouse when it's tipped over is bad enough, but Uncle Bert soon discovered another disconcerting fact. The thing had fallen onto its front so he couldn't get the door open.

He tried standing on the inside of the now horizontal door and moving the rest of the building with his shoulders. He soon figured out that was hopeless since the door opened toward the inside, and no amount of pushing was going to do any good. No amount of hollering was going to accomplish anything either, since he was home alone at the time.

Bert knew he was in trouble. He also knew, though, that his troubles were just beginning. That dang wife of his would have no end of fun teasing him about the time he locked himself in the outhouse by tipping it over with him in it.

Uncle Bert figured he'd hear about that incident at every family reunion and every time they had company. He knew she'd tell all the neighbors, and he'd never hear the end of it.

He sort of half crouched and half stood in that tipped-over outhouse contemplating the raw deal that fate had dealt him.

Now a raw deal is one thing, but downright tradgedy is quite another. The full realization of his situation occured to Bert when he saw that little curl of smoke drift into the outhouse from one corner down on the ground. That doggone fire had crept over to the outhouse and was fixin' to catch it all ablaze.

Dyin' in an outhouse was not Uncle Bert's idea of the ideal way to go. Visions of his neighbors snickering over his manner of death flashed momentairly through his mind. He got to thinkin' that maybe they'd even be considering that at his funeral. Even worse, they might be thinking of that when they buried him!

Things had suddenly gotten desperate, and an answer had to be forthcoming."

Apparently there is some sort of adrendlin-like enzyme in the human body

(58)

that responds to the possibility of death in an outhouse, for Ruth told me of how her Uncle Bert found the strength to match the seriousness of the problem. He managed to break enough of the siding off that structure to crawl out and escape. Bert was one happy man, being out of that now smoke-filled outhouse.

"Uncle Bert got the fire stomped out and saved that broken-down old thing from burning to the ground. Fact is, he was careful to patch the hole up that he'd made and stood the thing back up before Aunt Ida got home. He figured she'd talk about the situation only if she knew about it."

"So, I asked, "Did he ever tell your aunt about what happened that day?"

"Oh, yea, but it was a long time later. In fact, they had left Carroll before he did. He figured she wouldn't be so apt to make a lot of noise about it if she wasn't around the friends and neighbors she knew real well."

So, dear reader, don't get to actin' too smug about that decrepit-looking old outhouse on page 54. After all, has the condition of your nice inside bathroom ever saved your life?

One Peek Too Many

CHAPTER VIII

LAURA'S REVENGE

country grade school south of Ottumwa in Wapello County had, like the hundreds of other schoolhouses in Iowa, its outhouses. Unlike most, however, these were in two separate sections of the same small building instead of in two different buildings.

That arrangement was done on occasion since it was a little cheaper to build one building instead of two.

It was necessary, of course, that the two sections be kept rigidly separated. The wall between the two sections of this particular outhouse was of boards cut from some of the native lumber there in Wapello County, from down on the Des Moines River.

Time and the elements conspired to twist and to warp those boards until a couple of them separated

(61)

enough that the boys could take advantage of the situation.

The girls suspected that those boys were in the practice of peeking when they had an opportunity. Those suspicions were confirmed one day when an eighth grade girl heard two of the seventh grade boys talking about it. That situation irritated her and the other girls enough that they got real steamed over the whole thing.

The girls' complaints to the teacher helped the situation somewhat. She made a rule that the boys couldn't use their outhouse whenever one of the girls was in the girls' half.

The reduced number of opportunities for some peeking just made the whole thing that much more of a challenge for the boys. They begin to apply their creative energies toward the goal of getting to peek that much more often.

The teacher, Miss Vance, wasn't able to control things quite so well at recess or at those times before or after school, so that's when the boys would watch the outhouse carefully. When one of the girls went in there, that was their signal to rush into the other half and peek.

The girls realized, then, that some more direct action was necessary. They got their heads together and came up with a plan.

The scheme that the girls came up with was one they decided not even to share with Miss Vance. They were afraid that she would veto the whole idea. It was a good plan and they sure didn't want to have to give it up.

One of the girls swiped her brother's squirt gun and filled it up with vinegar from home. She hid it in her lunch bucket and made off with it to school one day.

When this gal got to school, she hid that weapon out there in the outhouse, up over the door.

She and the other girls that were in on the scheme could hardly wait for morning recess. This was to be the day of their revenge and the minutes drug by as if time had almost slowed to a stop. All chances of learning anything that morning were gone as each of the girls savored the thought of teaching those boys a good lesson. This was to be the day!

Time brings all things, of course, even 10:30 when it seemed that recess time would never arrive. Some of the girls were totally unaware of what was going on as all the children trooped out of the room for their recess. The older girls were having trouble enough keeping the plan secret. They knew that the little girls would get so excited about it that they would let the cat out of the bag within a few minutes.

The plan was for the Simpson girl to spring the trap. After about five minutes into the recess period, she set the whole process in motion. Laura Simpson waited until it was her turn "at bat" in their ball game. She, of course, had the attention of the whole gang of kids at that time. While there at the center of attention, Laura made the announcement that she was going to make a trip up to the outhouse.

Sure enough, it was all working. She no sooner entered that door, when one of the boys ducked into the boys' half of that building. Laura was giggling so much she was afraid that the boy would hear her and realize that something was afoot. Apparently, however, he was blissfully ignorant of the painful fate awaiting him.

Laura stood off to the side a little but was watching that space between those two boards very carefully. She had that vinegar-filled squirt gun all primed up and ready to go.

And there it was! An eye was peeking through that crack between those two boards into the girls' side. Laura hesitated only a few moment as she relished this opportunity to wreck her revenge on that nasty boy on the other side of the wall.

Laura put that squirt gun up to the crack in the wall and gave the trigger a couple good pumps. The piercing yelp that came out of that outhouse not only broke up the baseball game but roused the teacher from her desk. When she rushed to the door of the school to investigate, she was surprised to see a boy come running out of the outhouse, hollering like he'd been snake bit. He came crashing across the playground to the

schoolhouse. Miss Vance met him at the doorway and took his hands away from his face in an attempt to determine what the lad's problem was. He, in turn, kept howling and crying about his eye.

Miss Vance didn't know if he had stuck something in his eye, if he'd been stung, or whatever. She knew it was something very, very real, though. She could see that the eye was already red and swollen from whatever had happened to it there in the outhouse.

Miss Vance, not knowing what the problem was, sure didn't know a solution. She reasoned, however, that it sure wouldn't hurt if she washed the eye well. She quickly grabbed the dipper out of the water bucket and threw several dippers full into the lad's face.

That, of course, was a fortunate decision on her part. Her rinsing that eye out well undoubtedly prevented permanent damage.

Within a few minutes after Miss Vance washed his eye out, he calmed down enough that he was able to talk. By this time, Miss Vance was determined to get to the bottom of what had happened. At first the boy was reluctant to 'fess up as to what had transpiried out in that outhouse. Laura realized by that time that she had come close to seriously hurting the boy and was a pretty contrite little girl. She told Miss Vance the whole story.

(66)

She was chastised thoroughly for what she did. He was, in turn, rewarded with the opportunity to stay in from recess for two full weeks. To add injury to insult, that lad knew that when he got home that night he'd also feel the sting of a willow whip. He wasn't sure what his father's attitude would be about peeking into the girls' side of the outhouse, but he was abundantly aware of what he'd think about his kid getting into trouble at school.

Since no permanent damage was done either to the boy's eye or his backside when he got home that evening, Miss Vance let the whole matter slide.

One permanent result of the incident was that the boys grew wary enough to put an end to the peeking foolishness.

Jesse and Wilbert's Target

CHAPTER IX

THOSE DANG BOYS

rian Mitchell lived in a little crossroads community in Black Hawk County. He was a middle-aged man during these years in the early 1920s.

Brian and Mrs. Mitchell had raised their family and were looking forward to a life freed of the excitement and turmoil of raising kids. After having their own three girls and a boy, the Mitchells were ready for some peace and quiet.

In fact, that's just about how things went for awhile after their youngest left home. Unfor-

tunately, though, things weren't to prove to be quite so peaceful as they had hoped. Mrs. Mitchell's younger sister had two boys who were getting into trouble all the time in Waterloo where they lived.

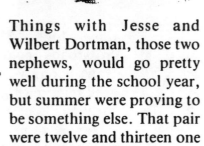

Things with Jesse and Wilbert Dortman, those two nephews, would go pretty well during the school year, but summer were proving to be something else. That pair were twelve and thirteen one summer and found themselves in one pickle after the other during that particular summer in Waterloo. The boys weren't bad boys but had so much energy it just got 'em into lots of hot water.

At first the problems that Jesse and Wilbert got into were pretty minor stuff. As the summer wore on, however, it got more and more serious. A couple of times a policeman brought the boys home after their escapades.

Mr. and Mrs. Dortman struggled through that summer with that bad-luck pair but resolved to come up with a solution for the next year. They knew these boys would be bitin' off more than they could chew unless something drastic was done to nip their tendency for trouble right in the bud.

The solution to the problem occurred to Mrs. Dortman one day just before school was to let out for the year again.

"Let's get Joyce and Brian to keep those boys this summer. They would have fewer chances to get into trouble if they were out of town and away from their friends."

Well, the idea wasn't exactly greeted by Brian and Mrs. Mitchell with a lot of enthusism' but after all, they were kin. If they could help they'd give it a try.

So the day school was out, that pair of young fellows were packed into the car and hauled to the Mitchell home.

The arrangement was that the boys were to help Brian with chores around the place in exchange for their board and room. Since the Mitchells had a little acreage with a few sheep and hogs, there were plenty of those chores to do. Brian was also awfully busy that summer tearing down the remains of an old barn. He was going to use the material to build a new one. He figured he could probably use those boys in doing that job.

Brian might never had heard the expression that goes to the effect:

> *"One boy is worth one boy.*
> *Two boys are worth half a boy,*
> *and three boys aren't worth*
> *anything at all."*

And that's just about all that Brian got out of that pair - half a boy's worth.

The Mitchells still had an outhouse in those days. It was about as common an outhouse as you'd hope to find. Those boys made it pretty distinctive one day, though.

It all started when Brian dusted off an old single shot .22 rifle his own boy had had when he was younger. He got that rifle all cleaned up, gave Jesse and Wilbert some instructions on what not to shoot, and turned 'em loose. That was almost his undoing.

Brian got pretty busy working on that barn, and it didn't occur to him those boys would bear some pretty close watching with that .22 rifle. He should have known that those lads would eventually get around to painting a round target on something to use for target practice.

The boys found the perfect thing to paint their target on. It was the back of that outhouse. The back wall of that building was a nice smooth surface, 'bout seven feet high and four feet wide. They were right proud of that pretty target with the alternating red and white circles, one within the other. Neither one of the two knew what an "official target" was supposed to be, but they wanted an "official" target for their practicing, and that's whey they had.

Jesse and Wilbert got into their target project with a whole lot more enthusiasm than good sense. In their eagarness to try that new game, they forgot to watch very closely that well-worn path between the outhouse and the back door of the house. By the time those boys got that rifle all loaded up, they didn't realize that Brian had stepped out there for a spell.

Brian was settin' there jus' mindin' his own business when the first bullet came flying through the outhouse. At first he couldn't quite figure out what was happening. All he heard was a couple of sharp cracks. It was a minute or two before he noticed the bullet hole in the door in front of him and just to his left. It was then he realized those sharp cracks he heard were the sound of the bullet going through the back wall and the front door of that tiny building he was occupying.

Next thing Brian knew, another hole appeared like magic a little above the first. One instant it wasn't there, the next instant it was. Just about then Brian realized that those were bullets flying past him, he let out a wild whoop of surprise, fear and anger. He no sooner did that when another bullet slammed past him, just missing his ear by a couple of inches.

Brian was mentally calculating how long it would take those boys to reload that single shot rifle as he frantically gathered up those shoulder straps on his bib overalls so he could escape from that outhouse that was rapidly threatening to be a death trap. As luck would have it, the little brass eye on the end of one of those straps got hung up on a nail. That delayed his escape for a few seconds. It was during those few seconds that he saw that old Montgomery Ward catalog jump a little bit as a bullet plowed into it all the way to page 314.

 Not particularly anxious to see where the next bullet was going to be hitting, Brian literally threw himself out the door, leaving half his bib overalls hanging on that nail and the other half flapping behind him as he fled for the house.

Brian's luck, bad as it was, held for him. Mrs. Crocker, their next-door neighbor, was out hanging up her wash when Brian made his hastly exit. She knew nothing about the circumstances of

Brian's dilemma. All she knew was the neighborhood was obviously going downhill when Brian Mitchell was running around the yard half dressed in broad daylight.

You better believe there were some mighty pointed remarks that day about responsibility, good sense, and watchin' out for the other feller's safety. All this, of course, while the rifle was being packed away again.

Jesse and Wilbert's antics took a real toll on the Mitchells, and they were complaining one day to a couple of neighbors about "those dang boys" who seemed to know nothing but trouble. Mrs. Crocker heard about these complaints. With a little sniff and a toss of her head, Mrs. Crocker delivered her own opinion on the situation. Her thoughts on the matter were inspired by her recollection of the day that Brian Mitchell was flyin' across the yard with half a pair of bib overalls on.

"Why, I saw him one day a comin' out of their outhouse just 'bout half dressed in the rattiest-lookin' overalls you'd ever hope to see.

I don't know much 'bout rais' boys, never havin' had any of my own, but I do know they need a good example set for 'em. I'm not real sure that Brian Mitchell is much of a model for growing boys."

The source of this story didn't know what happened to those two boys. My guess is, though, that they never used an outhouse for target practice anymore.

The Replacement Outhouse
After Eunice's Episode with the Monster

CHAPTER X

THE ATTACK

ike Sommer had a house in a little settlement east of Council Bluffs in 1913. Like most of the neighbors, Mike and Eunice Sommer still had an outhouse. Some of the folks in the area had inside bathrooms but not enough of them that the idea had even occured to Mike and Eunice yet.

Mike and Eunice were young, barely out of their teens when they married and settled there on that acreage. He was an enthusiastic deer hunter and would get a deer or two every fall. Mike wasn't what you'd call a sport hunter. He hunted because it was a lot cheaper than buying beef for the table. Bagging a deer in those days was a lot bigger deal than doing so now. There were a lot fewer of them in 1913 than there are today. Getting a deer was somewhat of a newsworthy accomplishment back then.

One of his hunting buddies was more of a trophy hunter and infected Mike with the bug for hunting for trophy buck one year. As luck would have it, that was also the year that Mike happened to bag a nice large buck. His buddy convinced him

that he should have the head mounted. Well, after Mike found out what it was going to cost to do that, he figured he'd just have the hide tanned instead. He decided that hide would make a nice rug for in front of the fireplace.

The day when the fellows got home and got their deer cleaned up, Mike got to wondering where he was going to stash that hide where the mice wouldn't be getting to it and where Eunice wouldn't see it. He kind of hoped to keep that thing hid so he could surprise her with a nice fireplace rug come spring when it was her birthday.

That storage place seemed kind of an insoluble problem until the perfect place occurred to him. He'd just sort of roll it up into a bundle and hang it up near the ceiling of the outhouse. He figured those pesky mice couldn't get to it up there and Eunice probably wouldn't look up there either or accidently see it in the darkness of that outhouse ceiling. Besides that, it would be nice and cool up there so the hide wouldn't spoil while he was waiting for the hide man to come from Omaha. Mike was real proud of himself for thinking of that.

(78)

Everything almost worked out according to plan. He hung that hide up there, and it was just perfect. He knew the hide man would be around in about three weeks. It hadn't gotten cold enough yet that the hide would freeze. It was just like a refrigerator out there, so it was all working out alright. Eunice must have gone in and out of that outbuilding three or four dozen times and never once saw that hide hanging up near the ceiling.

In fact, it was all going just fine up until a couple of days before the hide man was due to come and pick up that nice deerhide.

It was on a Thursday morning and Eunice was home alone, Mike being off to work, and all. She took a trip out to that outhouse. That's when it all happened.

One thing the reader ought to know about Eunice is that she was just a slip of a girl. She came nowhere close to weighing a hundred pounds and had the appearance of porcelain, what with her skin being so soft and white. She sure wasn't what you'd call a tomboy. Mike was in the habit of calling her a sissy, she being so small and fine featured. He didn't mind her being that way; he just enjoyed teasing her about it.

But back to the outhouse. Eunice stepped into that dark little room. It was always kind of dark in there, but on that day, it was especially so. The sun was hidden under some thick dark clouds and it was just one of those dark and dreary days. The inside of that outhouse was almost like at nighttime.

No sooner had Eunice stepped into that outhouse and shut the door when the cord holding that deerhide let go. Mike should have used rope. That  twine just wasn't up to the job. Eunice was thinking of neither twine or rope. All she knew was that as soon as she shut that door some large and hairy thing leapt upon her from out of the darkness, almost weighting her down to the floor. What with all the flailing around she was doing trying to escape, she had no way of knowing that it was her frantic jumping around that gave the impression that the thing, whatever it was, was attacking her.

Those next few moments were like an eternity for Eunice as she struggled with that monsterous animal that had attacked her. That less than 100 pounds of sissy-hood seemed to call, from the depths of her instincts, strengths she never even dreamed she had. With a couple of good smashes with her shoulders, Eunice Sommer tore a hole in the side of that outhouse and flung herself out of that little building. She was shocked to find herself out of there and still alive. She could see a small part of that large animal, still inside. Fearful that it would be on her in an instant, her eyes sought the ground for a weapon of some sort. Miraculously, she spied a five gallon can of fuel oil setting by the corner of the outhouse. She remembered Mike had had that out there for something or other. Eunice knew she had to gather her last ounce of strength to save herself before that beast leaped upon her again.

In an instant, Eunice picked up that heavy can of fuel oil and splashed it onto the outhouse. She knew she had some matches in the pocket of her apron. If she could get that building afire before that animal followed her out, she might yet be able to save herself from the jaws of that horrid animal.

It took just another couple of seconds to whip out those matches and set the building afire. Within seconds the flames were climbing high in the air and the animal had not yet come out. As the outhouse started to sag and crumble, Eunice knew she had won. Suddenly she felt small and weak again. In fact, her knees, wouldn't hold her up anymore as she sank to the ground and watched the last of the outhouse sink into the pit below. She saw what was left of that now fire-blackened beast half lying under all the ashes and coals.

By the time Mike got started for home for the evening, Eunice had gotten back into the house and had gotten herself prettied up again after her ordeal. She was surprised to find she was remarkabley free of any scratches, bites, and so forth. She really felt that she was fortunate that she had fared so well after that vicious attack by that large critter. She still hadn't figured out what kind of animal had jumped her. The only things she could think of were bears or some kind of large wildcat. She knew she had escaped, using her own strength and cunning. She was proud of that.

 When Mike pulled into the yard, the first thing he noticed was that the outhouse was missing. The next thing he knew, his wife was rushing from the house and throwing herself into his arms for safety and security. All that composure was gone now. Eunice just wanted Mike to take care of her and to protect her. Between sobs, she managed to tell him about the huge beast that attacked her.

As the full realization of what had happened occurred to Mike, he didn't know if he should be mad at her for destroying the outhouse or if she should be mad at him for putting that deerhide up near the ceiling of that outhouse. His solution was to sit down and start giggling.

That, of course, didn't seet too well with Eunice. Here she had barely escaped the cluthes of a ferocious animal and her husband laughs about it!

Well, it was Mike's turn to talk. He 'fessed up to having put that hide in there and explained that it had simply fallen on her.

Between laughs that he found it increasingly difficult to control, Mike pointed out to Eunice that she had set fire to the outhouse for no reason at all.

For the next three days there was this young couple near Council Bluffs that couldn't look at each other without breaking out into the giggles. As the years went by, they got over the giggles but never forgot the day of the great beast attack.

The Site of Story County's Earthquake

CHAPTER XI

THE HOMEMADE EARTHQUAKE

r. and Mrs. Orton Kelly and their two sons, Joe and Sean, lived on a farm between Ames and Nevada from 1914 til 1922. There was nothing particularly remarkable about the Kelly family or the Kelly farm except one Saturday morning in 1915 when it fell victim to an earthquake. Strangely enough, it was the only farm in the community that had an earthquake that day.

Orton worked the farm, and Mildred worked Orton. The two boys did the more important stuff like plinking frogs, skipping stones on the pools of water in the creek, and riding their broken-down pony on those rare occasions when they could catch him. The pony was good exercise for the boys 'cause they'd get so much of it in trying to catch that contrary critter. They'd just run themselves silly for an hour for a five minute ride until he'd just sit down and refuse to move another foot.

Joe and Sean were fully aware that adults and children were almost two different species and that the proper role of each was to say out of the hair of the other. As a result, those boys were not aware, until almost the last day, that Aunt Ida was coming by train from California to visit. It wasn't

that Aunt Ida's visit was such a big deal. It was just natural for Orton and Mildred to keep that sort of thing secret.

The prospect of Aunt Ida coming was met with mixed emotion by the boys. They had seen her only once or twice and didn't like her. They had learned most of what they knew about her from some cousins who knew her better. Those cousins were unanimous in their opinions that Aunt Ida was about the worst thing that had ever happened. She was a mean, vindictive, and ill-tempered tyrant.

Actually, Aunt Ida wasn't the boys' aunt at all. She was their great aunt. She was really Orton's aunt.

When the news about Aunt Ida broke, the boys noticed that neither of their parents seemed overwhelmed with joy about her coming either.

Finally the big day arrived. Aunt Ida got off the train and greeted the family cooly. The boys were a bit disappointed. She neither had horns nor breathed fire. She looked like any other old lady. It's hard telling how old she really was. To the boys, anyone over thirty as old.

Joe and Sean soon learned that appearances were deceiving. Aunt Ida's lack of horns or breath of fire meant nothing. She was the gosh-awfullest woman they had ever seen. All those reports from various cousins were wrong. She was much worse than the boys had been led to believe.

The boys soon developed the only possible strategy. They would avoid that tyrant in skirts at every possible occasion. Their dismay at having her visit grew into alarm and then panic when they found out she was there to study the possibility of moving in with the Kelly's. Such a possibility was too awful to even contemplate, but contemplate it they must.

It seems that Aunt Ida had taken a sudden and deep fear of earthquakes and was looking among her relatives for refuge outside of California. It didn't take long for the boys to figure that they could use that fear to their advantage. They decided that they should convince Aunt Ida that Ames and Nevada were virtual powder kegs in terms of the possibility of earthquakes. As they learned all they could about earthquakes, they were shocked to learn that a major earthquake in the U.S. had been right here in the Midwest and had been easily felt there at home. They learned about the New Madrid quake. This was uncommonly good news, of course. A bad quake in the Midwest was nothing short of a miracle, even it had been over a hundred years ago. If it could happen once, it could happen again.

During those times when contact with Aunt Ida was unavoidable, such as at meal times, those two boys would slip in a remark now and then about the New Madrid earthquake. Aunt Ida listened to them when they talked earthquakes, and it was about the only time she did. It was a delicate balancing act. They wanted to get in as much as they could about that quake, and the certainty of more to come. Yet they didn't want to overdo it for fear of it becoming obvious what they were doing. Their mission was to scare Aunt Ida off at all costs. The prospect of her living in their house was simply too catastrohpic to bear.

It was Sean who first came up with the idea of the rope on the outhouse. Those boys quickly leaped on that and put their plan into motion. They rigged up a thin wire to the outhouse that led off between a tree and a bush. Onto that, they tied a long hay rope. By pulling on that rope in a rhythmic manner, they could get that outhouse gently swaying back and forth. It took a lot of practice to get the outhouse swaying as they thought it probably would in an earthquake.

John and Sean decided that central Iowa would experience its earthquake on Saturday when they were home from school and could man that rope. They had each taken a turn on the rope and each inside the outhouse in their effort to fine tune the rocking action they wanted that outhouse to go through.

The prospect of having to man that rope all day Saturday, waiting for Aunt Ida to go out there was pretty bleak. There were so many other things to do on Saturday, they hated to waste it waiting around to rock Aunt Ida around. The alternative was, however, a lot worse. They knew they simply couldn't have that woman around all the time.

Fortune smiled on the boys, however. They were sitting up on that hillside with that rope in hand for only a couple of hours before Aunt Ida appeared at the back door. She walked straight for the outhouse and shut the door behind her. This was the big opportunity! This was the moment that could well determine the circumstances of the rest of their lives at home!

Joe had developed the finer hand at getting that outhouse rocking back and forth. Joe could make that outhouse sway with a slight circular action. It was Joe who was handling the rope up there on the hillside. As Joe was creating his one-outhouse earthquake, Sean went running down the hill hollering for all he was worth about the ground shaking and how the earthquake had done struck.

"We're having a sure-fire earthquake! Run for your lives, everybody!"

It was a go-for-broke strategy. After you create an earthquake and then go around hollering about it, you've just about played your whole hand. This was the moment of truth. This was the moment when Aunt Ida would either realize they had been attempting to drive her away or their scheme would work.

Aunt Ida came out of that outhouse as if she had

been shot. She was screaming something about packing her bags and getting her lazy nephew to haul her to the train depot. The flurry of activity around the Kelly farm was bewildering, even to the two that had caused it all.

(90)

Joe, Sean and Mildred found themselves alone as Orton took Aunt Ida to meet the train. The boys could hardly believe their good fortune. Aunt Ida was gone, apparently, for good. The threat of her moving in with them was gone. The boys didn't realize it, but so was some of the innocence of childhood gone.

Orton, a couple days later, ran across that hay rope up on the hillside. The boys knew that he knew and they figured they were in for a real good whoopin'. Orton stood and studied the rope while the guilty pair stood at rigid attention, held there with naked fear.

"You boys better get this good manilla rope back to the barn 'fore it gets rained on. Then come in for supper."

With an ever so slight smile, Orton Kelly turned and walked away to wash up for supper.

The boys looked at each other with a grin and decided that maybe parents weren't so bad after all.

John Sutter's Waterloo at Fort Dodge

CHAPTER XII

A PLAN THAT BACKFIRED

s I traveled around Iowa gathering these stories and photographing Iowa's vanishing outhouses, I learned a couple of interesting things. One of these was that a lot of memorable incidents about Iowa's outhouses had to do with tipping someone else's over. Of these, I liked best the ones when the aggrieved party would somehow turn the tables so that the tipper-overer ended up getting the worst end of the deal.

So when I started to hear this story, I was under the impression that it was one of that type. As it turns out, it isn't. The sneaky no-good bums doing the tipping emerged victorious. This story comes out of Fort Dodge and tells about what happened there back about 1900.

Those Halloweens in Fort Dodge were tough days for outhouse owners which included just about everybody. Come November first morning, about twenty-five percent of the buildings would be tipped over. It was, of course, the twenty-five percent that consisted of small buildings with a quarter-moon on the door, so it sure wasn't very serious.

It seems that the tradition was for groups of young fellows to go around on Halloween night tipping over outhouses, then wander around town the next day watching irate owners stand 'em back up. Tradition also dictated that a given outhouse tipper-overer would go to watch his particular victim upright the specific outhouse that he had tipped over the previous night. This was especially galling to the owner, to know his audience was the cause of his labors.

The common procedure was that the tipper would pretend that he had known nothing about that particular outhouse and the tipee to act like his audience wasn't the guy who did it. Everyone knew the charade was just that, but everyone played the game. After all, tradition is tradition, you know.

Well, John Sutter wasn't interested in playing that silly game. He wasn't about to turn all red-faced and huff and puff over getting his outhouse upright again while his tormenters watched and offered advice. He wasn't gonna give 'em that satisfaction. He didn't mind his outhouse gettin' tipped over nearly as much as he minded the culprits watching him go through the work of righting 'er up again.

John's plan was breathtakingly simple in theory. He just waited til almost two o'clock in the morning and went out and uprighted his outhouse which

was, by that time, lying on its side. He figured all the pranksters would be in bed by that time of the morning. John worked for almost an hour getting that thing up again and square on its base.

Along about three o'clock John got into bed, feeling good about messing up those vandals' plans. Come morning, he'd wander out early to work in the garden a little and watch the disappointment on the faces of whoever his tormentors proved to be.

John got up early and looked out. Sure enough, his outhouse was standing tall while all neighbors' were strewn about in disarray. It was a good feeling to have done all that, and the work in the night was simply an inconvenience for the pleasure of tormenting his tormenters.

So, out to the garden he went. It wasn't long before the two Jepson boys came wandering by, obviously confused about what they saw. They had expected to be able to offer John Sutter some helpful advice on how to straighten up that outhouse. But there it was, like it had been setting the previous night just before they tipped it over.

John, of course, engaged the pair in conversation. With his mouth he talked about the weather, the crops, and his neighbors bad luck with tipped-over outhouses. With his eyes, though, he was saying "So, you guys aren't so smart after all, are you?"

Those Jepson boys were disappointed. They figured that they had been outwitted on that one. The pair were just about to leave when a shriek from Mrs. Sutter changed all that. She had discovered her two brand new copper washtubs were missing. Those fancy new washtubs had hung there on the back wall of the house, and now they were gone. She came out and loudly announced that fact to John.

Those two boys then realized that fate had dealt them a pretty good hand, after all.

They waited around for quite a while before John discovered that those fancy new copper washtubs had been pitched down into the pit after the outhouse had been felled. Apparently John's lantern had failed to reveal that during those wee hours when he had propped the thing back up again. Now they were trapped down there again. The only way to retrieve them, of course, was to tip it over again and get 'em out.

That "So, you guys aren't so smart after all" look changed to pure loathing as John Sutter spent the next hour and a half turning red around his face and neck  and going through a lot of huffing and puffing to get that chore done.

The Jepson boys were, of course, more than helpful in offering neighborly advice on how to do the work.

The Burnt-Out Bee Hive's Replacement

CHAPTER XIII

THE BEEHIVE

t seems that sometimes folks just couldn't leave well enough alone and use outhouses only for outhouses. Often times some of those secondary uses that people would come up with would get them into lots of trouble.

Such was the case with the Wakefield outhouse at the edge of town in Dubuque in 1936.

Mr. and Mrs. Wakefield had four children, the oldest of these was a boy, age sixteen, in 1936. That boy, Alf, is now getting up in years, but he recalls the incident very well. He remembers the mess he got the family into that August.

"I 'spose if Pa knew all the trouble I was gonna be causin', he'd just made me get rid of all by bees."

"Bees?", I asked.

"Yep, I had some of the nicest beehives in Dubuque County. I made all my own hives and collected wild swarms to put in 'em. I really should have gotten into the bee business for a livin' since I liked to mess with 'em so much and was pretty good at it, too."

Alf then went on to tell me about the time he came up with what he figured was a brilliant idea.

"I wanted a hive like the University had. They had a hive with one wall built into a window there in their science building. They had that wall actually made out of the glass of that window. You could see those bees a workin' right there in the hive.

They'd have to take that glass out now and then and clean off the wax the bees would spread on it, but it was really somethin' to see.

"I figured we could have the same thing. Ma wouldn't let me have it in the house but said I could do it in the chicken coop or some other building."

"So what did you do?" I asked.

"I started to build one of those special hives in a window of the chicken coop but changed my mind and did it in the outhouse. I cut me a foot and a half square hole in the side wall of the outhouse and built a hive right on the outside, an' had a glass panel on the inside.

"It worked real well. You could see 'em real good, but they couldn't get on into the outhouse. Even Ma thought it was kind of a novelty to be able to set there and watch those bees work.

"I had that hive hangin' on the side of that outhouse from the fall of '35 'til August of '36. That summer was when I got into trouble with it.

"It was really my kid sister's fault over what happened."

"Let me guess." I interrupted. "The glass broke, and all those bees got into the outhouse."

"Yep, that's exactly what happened. Clare, she was out there and slammed that door to the outhouse too hard. The edgeboard fell off that door, and it swung right smack into that glass panel. It was in the middle of August and just about as hot as it could be. '36 was a terrible hot summer, you know.

"Well, those bees were real irritable from the weather, 'an when that glass broke, they jus' came 'aboilin' into the outhouse. Clare got out with only a sting or two, but I guess that outhouse was a pretty excitin' place there for a while.

"No one dared go out to try to do anything for the rest of the day. That night I was able to smoke those bees enough to drive 'em away from the broken glass, and I was fixin' to put another piece of glass in its place. I had laid my smoker down for a few minutes in order to go into the house for some tool or somethin'. You know how things can go. One thing led to another, 'an I didn't get back to that outhouse for 'bout an hour and a half."

"Did you get those bees back and the new glass up?" I asked.

Alf kind of chuckled before he answered my question.

"Ya know, I didn't. Fact is, I didn't need to do any more work on that outhouse at all."

"What do you mean?"

"The hive, the outhouse, the bees and everything else was gone."

"That's what they were. I had me one of those smokers that you put smouldering rags, in ya

(102)

know. Those rags must have spilled out of that smoker and lit there on that wood floor. All that was left was a big pile of ashes and hot coal when I went out there to continue my work. Everything was jus' plain gone. I couldn't even find my trace of that broken panel of glass.

"I'd done burned the outhouse down. I would have figured there'd 'a been some of the bees buzzin' around, all mad about it, but even they were gone.

"I didn't get in as much trouble with Ma and Pa as I figured I would. Clare and me, we had to build a new outhouse, though. Pa wouldn't turn a hand to help us. He told us that we had burned it down all alone, so we could build a new one all by ourselves."

Michael Noble's In-House Outhouse

CHAPTER XIV

REMODELING THE OUTHOUSE

 owa is well known for its commitment to education. That commitment is probably illustrated with the Michael Noble outhouse better than at any other structure in the state.

Michael lived near Muscatine down along the creek that flows into the Mississippi River, not too far south of town. Along with Michael there in that modest home were his two nephews and one niece in that fairly large, but modest home. These kids were all somewhere between the ages of ten and seventeen when this happened in 1932.

The Noble outhouse was built right up against the house. Michael was not one to enjoy long trips out to the house "out back" when there was a bunch of snow on the ground and the wind was blowing.

Michael Nobel had gotten very little formal education in his youth. He sure didn't let that slow him down, though. He had taught himself how to read after he grew up. He was an accomplished reader, not being content to "just get by." He became an avid student on a wide variety of subjects and continued to be for the rest of his life.

Like many folks, Michael kept some reading material there in the outhouse. In most homes, that reading material was pretty much limited to a couple of out-of-date magazines and the ever-present mail-order catalog. In some, it was limited to that catalog.

The outhouse at the Noble home was considerably different. That shelf along the sidewall held a wide variety of lots of different kinds of books and magazines. Michael would periodically lecture those kids on the subject.

"There's no point in just setting there wasting your time. Put it to good use and get some reading done. You'll find all kinds of educational things in those books and magazines out there."

Michael's love of reading was infectious. The kids did use that collection of books and stuff there in that outhouse.

Michael insisted on those kids working hard and pulling their own weight there on the farm. There was, of course, no end of work to be done. But he wouldn't begrudge their reading time, almost regardless of when or where they choose to do it.

It soon became apparent that four avid readers, each with their own and changing interests, ended up collecting a bewildering array of books, pamphlets, magazines, etc. That shelf in the outhouse soon proved to be inadequate.

Michael's solution to the shelf problem by putting another one above it and one below it was an answer for a while. Soon, however, Jason's interest in music exhausted those extra shelves. He had gotten a whole bunch of used books from a neighbor and promptly drug most of them out to the

outhouse. That was Jason's favorite place to read, so that's where he wanted his collection of books about his new love, music.

Along about the same time, Annie got all involved in photography.

The library there in Muscatine had been given a large collection of books from an estate. These included a bunch of stuff on photography. The librarian knew that Annie was on a photography binge so gave most of those to her. Annie drug those home as if they were the pearls of wisdom of the ages. Well, you know where a lot of them went.

Pretty soon there were so many books out in the outhouse, there wasn't hardly any room for a person to get in there.

It was at that time that Michael realized that simply more shelves wasn't the answer, and that something more drastic had to be done. Either the outhouse had to go, or the books did.

Good sense prevailed and some minor modifications were made. A doorway was cut through the wall of the house leading into the outhouse. A cement floor was poured under it, the little house was insulated, a window installed where the door had been and the walls covered with nice new pine boards.

By the time Michael and the boys got done with their project, that little building no more looked like an outhouse than it did a chicken coop. The Noble family had 'em a fine little library, right off the living room.

Of course, that precipitated another problem. They had to build a new outhouse.

Annie was telling me all about the situation. When I was talking to her about this, she suddenly burst out laughing about something she recalled.

"You know, Uncle Michael was the dangest man I have even seen. You know what he told us after he and my brothers got that new outhouse built?"

"What?" I asked.

"He said 'Now, we got that shelf out there in the new outhouse. You better put some reading materials out there. There's no sense in just setting there wasting your time, you know' ".

Ruth's Mistake

CHAPTER XV

THE STONE OUTHOUSE

yle and Ruth Shaw came to Scott County and bought the old Farnham place near Davenport. The Shaws were pretty well-fixed, financially. Lyle had worked for many years in an office high above the streets of Chicago. He retired in 1898 and was determined to become a gentleman farmer. He was plumb full of city life and was looking forward to living on that farm near Davenport.

Neither Lyle nor Ruth knew the first thing about living in the country, but that didn't reduce their enthusiasm for the idea.

Lyle had made several trips to Davenport before that big day in '98 when the couple moved. Lyle knew the place was pretty well run down. He had, in fact, already had some fellows out to the place to start some building projects. Almong these was a new barn, a lot of tree planting, and some fence work.

When Ruth got there and had a chance to look at the place more carefully, she was appalled at the condition of the outhouse. She was willing to make some concessions to life in the country but putting up with that broken down old outhouse wasn't one of them.

"Lyle, you've simply got to do something about the little-house-out-back. It is in absolutely terrible shape, and I'm not going to put up with it for a minute."

Lyle had a dozen projects going on at once and had no time to worry about the outhouse and told her so. He told her that if she was so all-fired excited about that she could use one of the workers and some of the building materials he had bought for the various projects. She could just have the man build a new one.

So, that's what she did. She enlisted one of the men Lyle had hired and told him to build a new outhouse. She told him exactly where she wanted it and what it was to be like.

Al was a pretty good carpenter and figured he could do that job just fine.

Everything went along okay for a while. Al dug the pit and proceeded to put together the framework for the new structure.

It didn't take Ruth long to see that Al hadn't gotten the message. She wanted a first-class outhouse, not one of those rickety old wooden ones.

"Al, you just take some of those rocks that Mr.

Shaw had hauled out here for the foundation of the new barn and build it out of those. I want the outhouse to be substantial and I want it to match the limestone on the summer kitchen here."

"But, Mrs. Shaw, I don't think you'd . . . . ."

"Never mind, Al. Just do it."

Now, Al wasn't anybody's fool. He'd moved enough outhouses in his life that he knew you couldn't move a stone one. His next attempt to point out that a body doesn't go around building stone outhouses was met with the same response. She didn't have the foggiest idea of how not to build an outhouse but wouldn't listen. She wanted that stone outhouse, and that was all there was to it.

When Al appealed to Mr. Shaw with his problem, he was simply brushed aside with a wave of his hand and told Al to do whatever she wanted.

Al's sharing his problem with the other workers got him nowhere. They'd never heard tell of such a situation. They couldn't figure out how a man would move one of them but offered no advice at all on how to handle Mrs. Shaw.

"If'n I wuz you, Al, I'd jus' go 'head 'an build her her crazy outhouse. You ain't the one that's goin' have to move it, ya know."

So Al went ahead and did it. That outhouse was five feet wide and seven feet long. It was eight feet

(114)

to the roof line. It had a solid stone foundation and footing. Al figured it weighed about eight tons and was very thoroughly anchored to the ground.

It didn't take long for the word to get around the community. The folks around the area knew that permanent-placed outhouses involved the need to clean them out, and that well-heeled man from Chicago sure wasn't going to be doing that.

A lot of folks in the community just couldn't believe all that was going on. The Shaw place suddenly became awfully popular as people would stop in there to ask directions. Each of those direction seekers seemed to be a whole lot more interested in studying that new outhouse than in following the directions they came after.

Barroom discussions yielded several ideas on how a fellow would go about moving an eight-ton outhouse, but no one was confident that they could do it without breaking it up.

The Shaws, meanwhile, were blissfully unaware that Ruth had designed that flaw into the outhouse or of all the excitement in the community about it. It was much later that that realization struck home. It was then that Ruth realized why Al had been so resistant to building the outhouse the way she wanted it done.

Ruth's answer was simple and direct. She just changed that outhouse into a smokehouse and had a wooden outhouse built not too far away.

Sidney's Prison

CHAPTER XVI

THE LOCK-UP

t was what could have been a tragic situation up around Mason City in 1903. It all happened on a farm near that big curve in the Winnebago River north of town. Sidney Jarrsma owned that farm and had lived there for several years. Sidney was a single fellow. Oh, he'd had a couple of opportunities, years earlier, to get married. At the last minute, though, it seemed to Sidney to be more trouble than it was worth, so he didn't.

Sidney had no reason to farm on a very big scale. His needs were modest and he did just enough farming to provide an adequate living. He had both the outside and the inside work to do, so that took quite a bit of time.

Things were going pretty good for Sidney. He had settled into a pretty stable routine. He would be all alone there on the farm except for those rare occasions when he'd hire some extra help for a short period.

Sidney should have really gotten to town more than he did. He should have worked just a little bit harder to develop his social skills. Old Sidney was just plain hard to get along with. Besides that, maybe he wouldn't have had to almost lose his life in his outhouse. That incident was due to his contrary nature.

The man he got to work for him for a short time in the fall of '03 found Sidney particularly difficult to work with. The two clashed from the very first hour they were together. Things didn't get any better the rest of the day or the rest of the week.

Sidney was looking forward to Lester leaving, and Lester was anxious to see the last of Sidney. They got to arguing and fussing so much that Sidney was just about to the point of wondering if he couldn't get just as much done by himself if he didn't have to spend so much time fightin' over every little thing that came up.

Along about the ninth or tenth day that Lester was there, things got just intolerable. Lester decided he would be cutting out that very day. He wanted to do so at the most opportune time, however. He wanted his leaving to be a real problem for that old codger.

Lester was driving a team and wagonload of corn when he saw his opportunity. Sidney had stepped into the outhouse. Without hesitating, Lester reined in that team and backed the tailgate right up against the door of the outhouse.

That put Sidney in an awkard position. The door swung outward so he couldn't open it against that tailgate. Even as Lester unhitched the team, Sidney was banging on the door and hollering for Lester to let him out of there.

He might as well have saved his breath. Lester had found his opportune moment, and he wasn't about to let that contrary old man out at all. He simply turned the horses into the pasture, saddled up a riding horse for his pay, and left the country.

There weren't many outhouses around Mason City, or anywhere else in Iowa, that an average man couldn't kick apart from the inside if he had enough time. Those little structures weren't usually built very well. Unfortunately, Sidney's was put together to last. It was built of native lumber, and bolted instead of nailed. Those bolts were just rusty enough to make them impossible to turn by hand, yet still stout enough to withstand any pulling or pushing that Sidney could do. To make matters worse, Sidney was not a large man at all. He was a bit on the scrawny side. Between his slight frame and the outhouse's good stout frame, he was simply unable to get out.

No amount of hollering and thumping around on the inside of that outhouse was going to do any good. The nearest neighbor was almost a mile away.

Sidney thought wistfully of his house just a few yards away where he and that dang Lester had stood just an hour ago on the porch, arguing about something or other.

He tried everything. The outhouse was so small he couldn't even get a run at trying to bust the siding out with his shoulder.

It was the next day when Sidney realized how much trouble he was really in. He hadn't eaten, drank, or slept for a full day. It started to dawn on him that another couple of days in that outhouse could be the end of him. He was already getting awfully thirsty with the sun beating down on that little outhouse. To make matters worse, it got downright cold that first night, and it felt like it would that next one, too.

It was that second night that the idea occured to Sidney. It was too late to do anything about it then, because he couldn't see, but if he could last til dawn, he had a scheme. That was to pry a piece of 2 x 4 briding loose which he figured he could do. He calculated that that 2 x 4 was about four inches longer than the outhoue was wide. If he could get that pried loose, he could get one end against one wall down there by the floor. If he could then force the other end down, it would pop the siding off the building in the process.

Come dawn, Sidney put his plan into motion. He found that he could, indeed, pry that piece of 2 x 4 briding out, but it took almost all day to do so.

By the end of the second day, Sidney had about had it. He knew that his plan was his only hope, so he proceeded to force that 2 x 4 down, scraping that wall as he pounded on that board with his fists. When it got to tight to pound it with his fists, he wore out both his boots, using them as hammers to drive that upper end of the 2 x 4 down. It was working but seemed to take a long time to do it.

Sidney could see light as two of those nice wide pieces of siding buldged outward. The extra light in there revealed something he hadn't know about. There in the corner, hanging from the ceiling, was an old rusty part off a cornplanter.

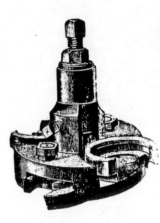

That piece of cornplanter was a lifesaver. With that he was able to continue hammering on the 2 x 4, forcing it lower and lower.

Suddenly, the most welcome sound Sidney had ever heard greeted his ears. It was the sound of those oak boards breaking from the strain of that 2 x 4. Sidney's renewed pounding did the trick. Those two boards popped loose. The interior of the outhouse was suddenly nice and bright. Sidney could see the grass out on the lawn, and feel the fresh air. Using one of those new-loosened pieces of siding as a pry bar, Sidney was able to remove others quickly. Within a few minutes time, he was able to wiggle out of his prison into the warm Iowa sunshine again.

The story of Sidney Jarrsma goes on to tell of how he went to the house for something to eat and

(122)

some water. Still chewing on some jerky, Sidney went to the barnlot to check on his horses. Apparently he was so glad to find his team safe and sound that he did not even notice until several hours later that a riding horse and saddle were gone. That dang Lester had taken off with one of his saddle horses, and the best saddle in the barn!

We don't know if Sidney set the law out on Lester or not. Apparently he didn't because neither Sidney nor any of the neighbors ever saw hide nor hair of the man who locked his boss in the outhouse up there north of Mason City.

Mr. O'Neil's 1929 Answer to His
Wife's Electrical Engineering in 1928

CHAPTER XVII

REDUCED TO ASHES

ire seems to have played an important role in the demise of lots of Iowa's outhouses. Maybe this is because they were often the site of childish mischief such as that first cigarette or a convenient place to play with matches.

The loss of the O'Neil outhouse to fire in 1928 wasn't due to kids, though. Mrs. O'Neil was able to claim full credit for that one. Fortunately, that farmstead south of Marshalltown suffered no other losses. No one got hurt and no other buildings burned, only the outhouse.

The O'Neils got "hooked up" to electricity in 1928. It was something of a big day, of course. While the O'Neils were a few years later than

(125)

some of their neighbors, they went whole hog. They figured if lights were good in the house, they were good in the barn, the summer kitchen, and even the outhouse. Mrs. O'Neil and her daughter were especially looking forward to a washing machine. They had had all the washing of clothes in an old wooden tub that they had wanted.

Now, lights in the house, and a washing machine was one thing, but lights in the outhouse was something else. It was the talk of the neighborhood for a while. Pat and Barbara O'Neil thought, though, that a light out there would be just as handy as all get out.

Mrs. O'Neil, unfortunately, had a theory about electricity. She became convinced that the electricity would leak out of any socket not plugged up with a light bulb. Furthermore it would leak out of any socket in which there was a burned-out bulb.

"Common sense will tell ya, Pat, that ya gotta have a good bulb in those sockets if you're gonna keep that 'lectricity from leakin' out."

Pat wasn't so sure of all that but figured that idea was as good as any other. So he went along with his wife's dangerous practice of stuffing rags in any socket whose bulb was burned out if she didn't have a spare one to screw into that empty socket. The O'Neils' daughter suggested they simple keep a good supply of bulbs on hand so they'd have one everytime one burned out on 'em. But you know how kids are. What do they know about electricity? Barbara lived to regret that she didn't listen to her daughter a little closer.

That practice of stuffing rags in those empty sockets was as dangerous as it was useless. Barbara had enough sense to stuff those rags down in them with a dry stick of wood, but not enough to refrain from doing it in the first place.

The O'Neil homestead got lucky for quite a while. The family enjoyed their new circumstances, blissfully unaware of the time bombs patiently waiting in half a dozen sockets in the house. The women really liked their new washer, and there were lights all over the place. No longer did they have to mess with those smelly old kerosene lamps.

 The inevitable happened one day along about suppertime. That wad of rags in the socket out in the outhouse got a little damp from some rain that leaked in the thing. Apparenlty that enabled the rags to conduct enough electricity to ignite the whole mess. That smouldering cloth ignited some wood nearby.

Pat was the first to see the smoke curling out from under the roof. By the time he rounded up a bucket and some water, that old outhouse was going real good.

Meanwhile the daughter called the rural fire fighting company that served that area, but that, too, was too late. By the time those fellows got to the O'Neil home, the outhouse was reduced to a rectangular shaped pile of ashes. Pat simply hadn't been able to keep up with his buckets of water pumped from the well there in the yard.

Now, having your outhouse burnt down was something like what we have to go thorugh these days when we get a speeding ticket. You not only have the expense of the situation, but have to put up with the little jokes and digs from just about

everyone you know. It wouldn't have been so bad for the O'Neils, except that outhouse had attracted so much attention earlier, what with the electric light in it and all.

On top of that, the chief of the fire company came calling about a week later. He had some pointed words to share with Mrs. O'Neil about stuffing rags in empty sockets. The chief and Mrs. O'Neil, in fact, took a tour of the house checking for any sockets that had any rags in them yet.

Mrs. O'Neil's daughter couldn't help but smile when the chief suggested that if they insisted on keeping the electricity from leaking out, they had better get a good supply of light bulbs.

The Harper Decoy Back Home Again

CHAPTER XVIII

THE OUTHOUSE ISSUE

t's hard for us today to relate to some of the issues that dominated the politics in our small towns many years ago. For instance, one of the small villages near Des Moines found itself embroiled in the issue of what to do about the annual problem of the good citizens finding an outhouse in the square every morning after Halloween.

The times were easy enough back then between 1900 and 1910 that the folks in town could concern themselves with such minor questions.

It wouldn't have become such a hot issue if one of the contestants for the upcoming mayoral race hadn't decided to make a big deal out of it. He promised that he'd bring an end to that practice if he got elected. In the absense of any competing issue of any significance, the outhouse one became the center piece of the campaign.

That was kind of an interesting subject, so many of the citizens got to debating the issue pretty heatedly. Well, after that, the mayoral candidates didn't have any choice. Each of them had to try to outdo the other in pointing out how they would solve the problem better than the other.

Fortunately for this story, the fellow who brought the whole issue up in the first place won the election. He would have just as soon forgotton the outhouse question after he got into office. He found out the mayoring business was a lot bigger than blustery compaigning about outhouses in the square.

(132)

Several of the voters weren't ready to forget it, though. They reminded His Honor of those pre-election campaign promises.

So the new mayor sat down with the town marshall along about the middle of October and let

him know in no uncertain terms that their jobs might well depend on bringing an end to that foolishness of the local kids bringing an outhouse to the square come Halloween in a couple of weeks.

The Marshall didn't need his mission explained in any clearer terms. He assured the mayor that he'd do his part. Those two fellows then combed through the city ordinances to find as many things that they could to bring gainst any one who put their jobs on the line by dragging one of confounded outhouses to the square that Halloween.

Meanwhile, of course, some of the local boys were doing their own planning along those lines. They knew that as much fun as doing that had been in the past, this year it was really going to be a goal worth pursuing. If the new mayor wanted to make a big deal of it, they'd help.

The frequency of comments by the citizens increased as Halloween drew closer. Any hopes that the mayor might have had that it was a dead issue were dashed. He knew he had to rise to the challenge on this one.

The big night came. Both the mayor and the town marshall were in the mayor's 1905 Cadallic. That car could really go and could easily outrun any delivery truck or horse-drawn wagon in the county.

The two fellows cruised around the square, starting early in the evening. The mayor knew that  anyone foolish enough to try it this year wouldn't do it early, but he wanted the folks to know he was giving that problem its just attention. He wanted them to know that the solution to that problem was due to him being in office.

Along about midnight or so the pair found themselves alone there, but they were resolved to stay until the stores opened in the morning if that was necessary. this year there'd be no outhouse dumped in the square!

Things were pretty quiet until about two in the morning. Suddenly the two heard the creaking of a loaded farm wagon. As they strained their eyes, they could see the wagon along the far side of the square. The mayor was the first to speak.

(134)

"Let's let 'em start to unload it before we jump 'em. That way we got 'em red-handed. If they do get it unloaded, we can make 'em load it back up again before we lock 'em up for the night."

So the pair watched that wagon go the full length of the block. When it got to the end, it didn't stop. It just kept a goin' and disappeared around out of sight. This was a bit unexpected, but the mayor started up his car and quietly drove around there to see what was going on. By this time, the wagon was a good block away from the square and was going along at a pretty good clip.

"What's those boys up to? Why didn't they stop and start unloadin' that outhouse like you figured they would?" asked the Marshall.

His Honor couldn't answer that question, but he was going to find out what those hoodlums were up to, so he gave chase.

That wagon didn't have a chance. The Cadallic was on them within another half block.

Investigation revealed that the wagon was occupied by Ted Harper and Josh Kidde. They acted real surprised and innocent when the mayor and marshall appeared out of nowhere and announced to the boys that they were under arrest.

"And, just whose outhouse is this?" demanded the mayor.

"Yeah, I'm sure the owner will have some charges to press over this," piped in the Marshall.

After all, the pair had caught these two after staying up most of the night and the marshall had no intention to miss out on some of the credit.

"Why, it's ours," replied Ted Harper. "When I was on my way home tonight I seen it laying along the road so me and Josh jus' gathered it up to take it home. Some no-good scoundrel took our outhouse and it's lucky we happened onto it the way we did."

The marshall had himself all puffed up pretty good so his badge on his chest would show off good. As he studied that outhouse, the air just seemed to drain outta him like he was a stuck ballon. He realized the lad was telling the truth. He knew that to be the Harper's outhouse.

The mayor was downright disappointed. There he thought he had 'em and he didn't after all. There was something, though, in Josh's eyes he didn't like. It was a twinkle that should not be in the eyes of anyone who was totally innocent.

The thought struck both the major and the marshall at the same time. Without a word, they jumped into that car and sped back to the square. That two blocks seemed like two miles as they hurried back, worried sick over what they might find.

Those two could not have come up with anything worse than what they found. There on one corner set the mayor's outhouse, and on the other was the marshall's.

The pair ran Josh and Ted down and hauled 'em to the jailhouse. They studied those books again to find something illegal about a man using his own outhouse as a decoy, but could find nothing. Along about dawn, they released the two and started frantically hunting down a truck to use to haul those outhouses out before people started to come downtown. It was no use. Those two outhouses still stood there for all to see come daybreak.

Fort Dodge's Temporary Prison

CHAPTER XIX

OUTWITTED IN AN OUTHOUSE

ne thing I have learned from the writing of this book is that a lot of stories about outhouses involve their getting tipped over, burnt down, or trapping their occupants one way or the other.

This one is a combination of the last two of these. At least it involves the last one and the threat of the other.

This incident was alleged to have happened on a farm near Fort Dodge in 1912. It started with the escape of a convict from his captor while they were traveling through the city.

Apparently the individual was thought to be capable of

virtually any crime and was known to be a very dangerous man. A local farmer involuntary provided him with both a rifle and a handgun when the culprit appeared on the farmer's doorstep and forced the frightened man to give him those weapons.

The convict was now armed as well as desperate. The word spread throughout the community rapidly and the residents were warned to be on the look out for the fugitive.

Mrs. Holmes was home alone that day, but wasn't particularly afraid because she was under the impression that the man was several miles to the north. She knew she was wrong when their dog set up a commotion. As Mrs. holmes stepped out onto the porch, she saw an armed man duck into the outhouse.

She knew that her life was in grave danger and she had better do something quickly. She figured her escape was impossible in that open area around the farm, so she choose to go on the offensive.

(140)

She grabbed up a gallon of gasoline that her husband had on the porch for cleaning the grease out of the windmill mechanism. She quietly came up from around behind the outhouse and slipped the latch into its eye there on the outside of the door.

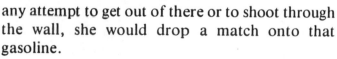

She immediately called to the man and told him that she knew who he was and that she was in the process of pouring gasoline all around the base of the outhouse. She warned him that if he made any attempt to get out of there or to shoot through the wall, she would drop a match onto that gasoline.

The surprised intruder didn't have to wonder if she was bluffing about the gasoline. The fumes were plenty strong enough in there, even as she talked.

"I hope you realize, Ma'am, that I can cover a lot of territory out there in a few seconds with this handgun. I can't tell exactly where you are out there, but I'll probably get you, so open that door. If you don't I can simply break it down, you know."

Her reply was a sobering one to the man inside.

"You can shoot all you want, and I know you can break the door down. But the first bullet better get me or I'll drop this match in the gas. The first movement I hear in there will prove to me you are going to try that door. The instant I hear you move at all, I'll drop the match."

This put the man in a pickle. He knew he probably wouldn't get her out the first shot. If he didn't, he'd be immediately engulfed in a ball of fire. He figured he could break that door with one good rush at it with his shoulder. He might then be able to roll out of the flames. But what if it took two cracks at that door? He'd never be able to make the second one.

Her voice again interrupted his thoughts.

"I'm sure you'll kill me without a second thought, so I have everything to lose and nothing to gain by hesitating. You make one tiny sound in there and I'll strike this match."

It was a hot day and the man knew as soon as that match ignited, those fumes would go with a roar. He could also tell, from her voice, that she was dead serious.

Almost an hour passed and the occupant of that outhouse hadn't yet dared to move but was getting sicker and sicker from the fumes. The thought also occured to him that she might be bluffing about the matches. She might not even have any matches. He had about made the decision to try that door in hopes that he could make it. Little did he know that in these few minutes prior to those thoughts, the woman's husband and a neighbor came riding up on horseback. She had silently signaled them to come on closer on foot and to be quiet.

With hand signals, she had conveyed to the two men what was going on. The husband then had hurridly gone to the house and returned with two rifles and a handgun.

The restive occupant of the outhouse knew it was all over when he heard the latch lift and a man's voice telling him there were now three people on the outside prepared to make a sieve out of the outhouse with rifles and instructing him to come out slowly without the guns. The voice told him that violation of either of those conditions would result in immediate riddling of the building.

A second man's voice confirmed that there were indeed, two men out there.

The now-sickened captive did come out and without his guns. He was quickly bound and put into a wagon to be taken to town.

As the men were leaving, Mrs. Holmes took the opportunity to tell the man that she had no matches.

Frank Thomas's Outhouse
With Roof Restored

CHAPTER XX

VINCENT'S BAD DAY

 rank Thomas down near Keokuk had a unique problem one day in July. Frank's place was chosen to be the meeting place for the Thomas family reunion on July 4th of that year.

The day proved to be notable, and for a reason totally unexpected. In fact, the events of that day in 1918 severely threathened the ability of many of the folks to get along very well after that. Unfortunately, a photograph was taken that fed the flames of contention that day.

The whole mess started with Frank's cousin, Vincent Bakeer from Chicago. The story goes that Vincent hadn't been totally sure that he wanted to come to that reunion in the first place. By

(145)

the time he got done with that day, he was convinced he would never go back. It was a day he never forgot.

An important element of this situation was Vincent's weight. He was approximately as big around  as he was tall. Vincent was pretty sensitive about his weight and resented it when anyone mentioned it or even behaved as if they were aware of it. He wasn't sensitive enough, however, to do anything about the problem, but that didn't make any difference. He just didn't want to hear about it.

Apparently Vincent had stepped into the outhouse. Like many others, it wasn't in the best of shape. Keeping an outhouse in tip-top condition is one of those things that it is easy to postpone. Frank had meant to build a new one before that reunion, but just didn't get it done in time.

As ill-luck would have it, Frank's Outhouse door opened inward. Vincent no sooner got inside and shut the door behind him when that old floor suddenly cracked and buckled under all that weight.

Fortunately, the floor didn't give way completely, but it had sure suffered a serious setback. Vincent grabbed that door handle in order to get out of that rickety old thing before it was too late. He discovered, however, that it was already too late. That floor had buckeled enough that the door was securely jammed shut.

Now, here was a dilemma. Vincent knew full well that his excessive weight had caused the problem. He needed help in getting out but to have hollered for help would have called everyone's attention to his situation. He could just hear those kids makin' all kinds of dumb comments about how he was so heavy he broke the floor.

Like Sidney Jarrsma in Chapter XVI, Vincent banged away at that door, but was still held captive. Too bad Frank and Sidney couldn't have traded outhouses. Sidney's problem was caused by his door opening outward and Vincent was trapped because Frank's opened inward.

It wasn't too long before all that commotion attracted the attention of the other fellows. It was just too mortifying for Vincent. He wasn't accustomed to those primitive outhouses in the first place, then to come out to Iowa and get locked in one was about more than he could bear. The reason for it made it that much more irritating.

Someone being locked in the outhouse was sufficiently exciting to attract the attention of a lot of the relatives. Several men gathered around to dry to get Vincent out, and the kids all came running to get in on the fun.

After all, it isn't everyday that such an exciting thing happened, you know.

To make matters worse, a group of ladies had gathered together to watch. They stood several yards away, of course.

Meanwhile, Vincent was getting madder and madder and not caring who knew it.

Frank would have been properly contrite, and would have offered plenty of apologies except for Vincent's behavior. Vincent was, after all, a guest and had no call to be saying some of the things he was saying about that outhouse, Frank's lack of care for it, and Iowa in general.

One of the fellows came up with the idea of rocking the outhouse back and forth, thinking the door might then open. All that did, however, was to twist the door jam enough to wedge it even tighter shut.

(148)

Several suggestions were offered by the men, a few by the ladies, and lots of 'em by the kids running around.

Finally Frank came up with the idea that the men adopted. It was probably the idea that was the most distasteful to Vincent.

The decision was to pry the roof off the building and help Vincent out with a rope strung over a stout tree limb overhead.

In practice, the "helping Vincent out" really consisted of pulling him out with a hoist hung from that limb. Frank claimed that he didn't mean for it to look that way, but it did. It looked just like they were pulling a frog out of a well. Frank's dangling from that hoist was what got on film.

For lots of years after that, copies of that photo kept making the rounds of the kinfolks. There are still alleged to be some tucked away in albums and in the bottom of trunks.

1918 was a long time ago, but yet today, the Chicago branch of the relationship and the Keokuk branch don't get along very well.

And it's all because of that dang outhouse.

CHAPTER XXI

REPOSSESSION

 had an opportunity to interview an elderly lady in Spencer to hear about the time her Great Uncle August got hauled away while he was innocently settin' in the outhouse. She had told me how he had bought the thing from a local carpenter, but hadn't paid for it.

When I went to meet with the lady, she told me her sister had vetoed the idea. Her sister didn't want "talk," you know. That incident was supposed to have happened in 1888.

Now, isn't that the dangest thing? Here it's been 101 years since Uncle August was roused from his duties there at Spencer by some dog-gone carpenter getting touchy about getting paid, and we can't hear the story!

Mark Reeves' High-Tech Outhouse

CHAPTER XXII

THE ELECTRIC FENCE

hen Mark Reeves went into Jefferson to get the makings for an electric fence in 1925, he did so over the objections of his wife. She just plain didn't want any of that electric fence foolishness on the place. She knew that you couldn't trust electricity, and it was totally unpredictable. She'd lived too long without it to learn to accept it at this late date.

Mrs. Reeves had made her point awfully strong, but it hadn't done any good. Mark saw that an electric fence was an ideal way to keep in those sheep he used to keep the weeds down around the buildings. He realized the advantages of that newfangled idea in that he could move that fence completely around in a few minutes. If he wanted

to concentrate those sheep around the barn he could do that easily. He could move 'em up around the corncrib or whereever else his fancy dictated. It was an exciting new idea and he was anxious to get right up there on the cutting edge of technology.

Mark hated to get his wife all steamed up over the issue but figured she'd get over that. So he came

home with those funny looking little skinny posts, the wire, and that formidable concoction of glass storage batteries to run the system.

There was, of course, the question of where to set those batteries. He wanted them out of the weather and yet convenient to work on, if necessary. Mark had heard enough stories about how lightning could hit an electric fence and really bust things up pretty good. So he decided to install those batteries in something real cheap like the outhouse, instead of the barn. He sure didn't want to have lightning coming into his nice barn burning it up.

Mark had the good judgment not to tell his wife about the lightning problem. He didn't think it would be of any usefulness to get her all worried about that. After all, the chance of lightning actually hitting his electric fence was only one out of two hundred. That fancy fence salesman with the 'spensive suit on had told him that. That man even went on to tell that he had a better chance of getting kicked by a horse than having his fence hit.

Well, since Mark never had been kicked by a horse, he figured he was pretty safe. Putting that rig in the outhouse was just being extra careful, of course.

Mrs. Reeves didn't say anything when she discovered he'd installed all that weird lookin' stuff in the outhouse, but she didn't like the idea.

After all the excitement on the Reeves' place during the next lightning storm had all died down, Mark was talking to that same salesman again. He asked him 'bout the chances of lightning hitting that fence at the same time his wife was in the outhouse. Turns out those chances were only one in ten thousand.

Well, there must have been nine thousand, nine hundred and ninety-nine customers before Mark

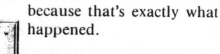

because that's exactly what happened.

Mrs. Reeves had gone out to that outhouse just as that old lightning started to flash back and forth in the sky. Somewhere out south of the

(155)

chicken coop one of those bolts tied into that nice new electric fence that was going to put Mark on the cutting edge of technology.

Mark didn't actually see what happened, and Mrs. Reeves was too shaken up to even remember. It must have been pretty exciting, though, in that outhouse. One whole side of that little building was blown clear off. The roof was split pretty bad, and the wood around where the wires came into the outhouse was badly charred.

When Mrs. Reeves came limping up the path to the house in a sort of daze, Mark got her lyin' down and stayed with her 'til he was assured she was alright.

By the time the storm was over and the sun was shinin' nice and bright again, Mark went on out to survey the damage.

He herded his pretty scared sheep up and got them into a pen. Next he rolled up what was left of the wire and set it in the shed. He put

(156)

those posts out in the garden where they would make fine tomato stakes.

Those beautiful glass batteries ended up as nests for his laying hens.

That was the end of Mark's playing around on the cutting edge of technology.

EPILOGUE

Like many Iowa outhouses, that one of Mark Reeves' near Jefferson now leans wearily against a tree. When you look at that old shack, it shows no evidence of the exciting day Mrs. Reeves got caught in there when lightning found its way into the building by way of an electric fence.

That curve in the road along the Des Moines River looks like any other curve in any other country road. Who would have thought that a harness salesman almost lost his job there because of a runaway outhouse on wheels?

Why couldn't that doctor outside of Sioux City trust his hired man enough to move the outhouse that day back in the 1940s? If he had, that outhouse might yet be alive today.

None of the children who attended P.S. #2 are alive today to remember any of the twelve outhouses that school had for its ten students. All that because the farmers kept insisting on stealing that schoolhouse.

Black Hawk County has survived the antics of the Dortman boys. Even their uncle lived through the day they used the outhouse for target practice. He sure wished he hadn't been in it, though.

The fate of the outhouse themselves has been varied. The one near Ames made it through the Great Earthquake of 1915, but the Sommers outhouse sure didn't make it though that day in 1913 when Eunice Sommers of Council Bluffs set 'er afire.

(159)

NEED A GIFT?
For

- Shower • Birthday • Mother's Day •
  • Anniversary • Christmas •

Turn Page For Order Form
(Order Now While Supply Lasts)

TO ORDER COPIES OF
IOWA'S VANISHING OUTHOUSES

Please send me _____ copies of **Iowa's Vanishing Outhouses** at $9.95 each. (Make checks payable to **QUIXOTE PRESS**.)

Name _____

Street _____

City_____State_____Zip Code_____

SEND ORDERS TO:
QUIXOTE PRESS
R.R. #4, Box 33B
Blvd. Station
Sioux City, Iowa 51109

TO ORDER COPIES OF
IOWA'S VANISHING OUTHOUSES

Please send me _____ copies of **Iowa's Vanishing Outhouses** at $9.95 each. (Make checks payable to **QUIXOTE PRESS**.)

Name _____

Street _____

City_____ ___State_____Zip Code_____

SEND ORDERS TO:
QUIXOTE PRESS
R.R. #4, Box 33B
Blvd. Station
Sioux City, Iowa 51109

If you have enjoyed this book, perhaps you would enjoy others from Quixote Press.

GHOSTS OF THE MISSISSIPPI RIVER
Mpls. to Dubuque by Bruce Carlson . . . . . paperback $9.95

GHOSTS OF THE MISSISSIPPI RIVER
Dubuque to Keokuk by Bruce Carlson . . . . paperback $9.95

GHOSTS OF THE MISSISSIPPI RIVER
Keokuk to St. Louis by Bruce Carlson . . . . paperback $9.95

GHOSTS OF JOHNSON COUNTY, IOWA
by Lori Erickson . . . . hardback $12.95

GHOSTS OF LINN COUNTY, IOWA
by Lori Erickson . . . . hardback $12.95

GHOSTS OF LEE COUNTY, IOWA
by Bruce Carlson . . . . hardback $12.00

GHOSTS OF DES MOINES COUNTY, IOWA
by Bruce Carlson . . . . hardback $12.00

GHOSTS OF SCOTT COUNTY, IOWA
by Bruce Carlson . . . . hardback $12.95

GHOSTS OF ROCK ISLAND COUNTY, ILLINOIS
by Bruce Carlson . . . . hardback $12.95

GHOSTS OF THE AMANA COLONIES
by Lori Erickson . . . . paperback $9.95

GHOSTS OF NORTHEAST IOWA
by Ruth Hein and Vicky Hinsenbrock . . . . paperback $9.95

GHOSTS OF POLK COUNTY, IOWA
by Tom Welch . . . . paperback $9.95

GHOSTS OF THE IOWA GREAT LAKES
by Bruce Carlson . . . . paperback $9.95

(Continued on Next Page)

MISSISSIPPI RIVER PO' FOLK
by Pat Wallace .... paperback $9.95

STRANGE FOLKS ALONG THE MISSISSIPPI
by Pat Wallace .... paperback $9.95

THE VANISHING OUTHOUSE OF IOWA
by Bruce Carlson .... paperback $9.95

THE VANISHING OUTHOUSE OF ILLINOIS
by Bruce Carlson .... paperback $9.95

THE VANISHING OUTHOUSE OF MINNESOTA
by Bruce Carlson . ... paperback $9.95

THE VANISHING OUTHOUSE OF WISCONSIN
by Bruce Carlson .... paperback $9.95

MISSISSIPPI RIVER COOKIN' BOOK
by Bruce Carlson .... paperback $11.95

IOWA'S ROAD KILL COOKBOOK
by Bruce Carlson .... paperback $7.95

HITCH HIKING AMERICA
by Bruce Carlson .... paperback $7.95

IOWA, THE LAND BETWEEN THE VOWELS
by Bruce Carlson .... paperback $9.95

GHOSTS OF SOUTHWEST MINNESOTA
by Ruth Hein........................ paperback $9.95

GHOSTS OF THE COAST OF MAINE
by Carole Olivieri Schulte .... paperback $9.95

INDEX

INDEX

Ames 85,87,159
ATTACK, THE 77
Bakeer.................................145
barn 71,91,112,113,126,154
baseball 64,65
bees 99,101,102,103
BEEHIVE, THE.........................99
BIG MOMENT, THE....................33
Black Hawk County 69,159
Boggs 52
bonfire 9,26,27
Boone 15,17
boots.................................26
Buffalo, N.Y. 13
buggy 18,20,21
bullet 73,74,144
Cadallic.............................134,135
California 86,87
cake..................................43
Carlson...............................33
carpenter 151
Carroll 55,56,59
Chicago 111,115,145,149
Cigarette.............................125
coffee 25
convict..........................139,140
Council Bluffs 77,83,159
Crocker...............................74
Davenport 23,111,112
Dedication...............................vi
deer 77,78
Demon Rum 14
Des Moines 41,131,159

Des Moines River 15,21,61
Dortman 70,71,159
Dubuque...............................99
earthquake...............85,87,88,89,90,159
education 105,106
ELECTRIC FENCE, THE..............153
electricity 126,127,128,129,154,159
Epilogue 159
Erie Leather Goods Company 13,20
fence...............99,112,153,154,156,159
fireplace 78
Foreward 9
Fort Dodge 93,94,139
fuel oil 81
frog.................................85
geese 34,40
guinea hens 34
GREAT SMOKED HAM ESCAPADE, THE41
Halloween.........23,25,26,27,93,131,133,134
ham 41,43,44,46,47
harness 13,14,17,18,19
Harper 136
hills 33,34
historian 27
hogs.................................71
Holland 23,26,27
holmes...........................140,143
HOMEMADE EARTHQUAKE, THE 85
hunting..........................34,77,78
ice cream 43
Iowa...............to numerous to mention
Jarrsma 117,122,147
Jefferson.......................153,159
Jepson 96,97
jerky 122

Kidde 136
Keokuk 145,149
lantern 16,96
LAURA'S REVENGE 61
library 108,109
LOCK UP, THE 117
Loess Hills 33,35
Marshall 133,135,136,137
Marshalltown 125
mayor 131,132,133,134,135,136,137
McQuire 15,18,19,20,21
Midwest 88
Mississippi River 105
Mitchell 69,70,71,72,74,75
Montgomery Ward 74
Muscatine 105,108
music 107
Nevada 85,87
New Madrid 88
New York 13
Nobel 105,106,109
oats 44
Omaha 78
O'Neil 125,126,127,128,129
ONLY SIX FEET 23
Oscar 35,36,37,38,39,40
Ottumwa 61
outhouse . . . . too numerous to mention
OUTHOUSE ISSUE, THE 131
OUTWITTED IN AN OUTHOUSE 139
overalls 73,75
Pearl 36
photograph 145,149
photography 108
physician 33

pie 43
PLAN THAT BACKFIRED, A 93
policeman 70
pony 85
REDUCED TO ASHES 125
Reeves 153,155,156,159
REMODELING THE OUTHOUSE 105
REPOSSESSION 151
rifle 72,73,74,140,143
saddle 123
SALESMAN, THE 13
school 49,50,51,61,62,63,67,70,159
Scott County 111
Shaw 111,113,115
sheep 71
sheriff 17
Simpson 64
Sioux City 33,159
smoke house 45,115
Sommer 77,80,159
Spencer 151
STONE OUTHOUSE, THE 111
summer kitchen 44,114,126
Superintendant of Schools 52
Sutter 94,96,97
teacher 65
Thomas 145
THOSE DANG BOYS 69
threshing 42
tractor 34
train 86
trapped 55
TWELVE OF 'EM 49
university 101
Vance, Miss 62,63,65,66,67
vandals 95

(170)

VINCENT'S BAD DAY 145
wagon 119
Wakefield 99
Wapello County 61
washtubs 96
Waterloo 70
WHY THE QUARTER-MOON? 29
windmill 141
Winnebago River 117
Yang 30
Yin 30
Year
  1500s 29
  1600s 29
  1880s 50
  1888 52,151
  1896 13,16
  1898 111,112
  1900 93,132
  1903 117,118
  1905 134
  1910 132
  1912 139
  1913 77
  1914 85
  1915 85,59
  1916 56
  1918 41,47,145,149
  1920s 23,26,69
  1922 85
  1925 153
  1928 125
  1932 106
  1936 99,101
  1940s 33,159
  1944 34
  1989 11